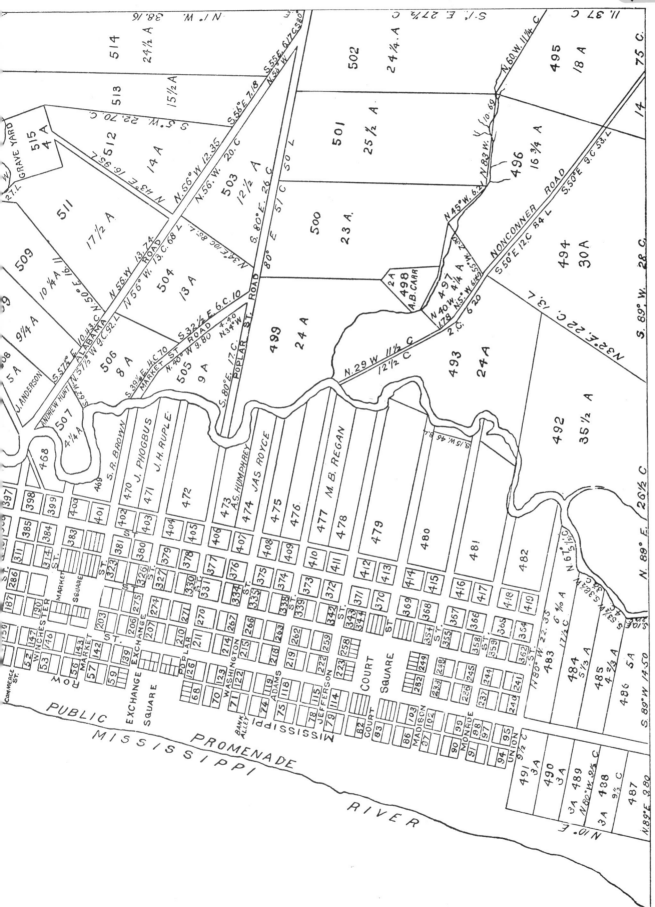

William Lawrence, 1819.

GOOD ABODE

*Men-Nopher, called Memphis
by the Greeks, meant,
to the early Egyptians,
"Good Abode"*

————————————

First Edition, First Printing

Library of Congress Catalog Card Number 83-50570
ISBN: 0-9604222-3-4
Printed in the United States by Towery Press, Inc.

GOOD ABODE

Nineteenth Century Architecture in Memphis and Shelby County, Tennessee

Written by Perre Magness
Photographs by Murray Riss

Published by
The Junior League of Memphis, Inc.
and
Towery Press, Inc.
1983

CONTENTS

CONTENTS	4
PREFACE	6
INTRODUCTION	7
CHRONOLOGY	14

MEMPHIS   15

■ COURT SQUARE   16
- Dr. D.T. Porter Building   18
- Tennessee Club   20

■ COTTON ROW   22

■ GAYOSO-PEABODY HISTORIC DISTRICT   26

■ DOWNTOWN CHURCHES
- Calvary Episcopal Church   28
- St. Peter's Roman Catholic Church   30
- St. Mary's Roman Catholic Church   32
- Trinity Lutheran Church   33
- First Methodist Church   34
- First Presbyterian Church   36
- Clayborn Temple   38

■ BEALE STREET   39
- First Baptist Beale Street   42
- Hunt-Phelan House   44

■ ADAMS AVENUE   47
- Magevney House   48
- First James Lee House   50
- John S. Toof House   51
- Fowlkes-Boyle House   52
- Mette House   54

■ VICTORIAN VILLAGE   55
- Mallory-Neely House   56
- Massey House   60
- Fontaine House   62

Lee-Fontaine Carriage House   65
Gingerbread Playhouse and Nineteenth Century Dollhouse   65
Goyer-Lee House   66
Mollie Fontaine Taylor House   71
Pillow-McIntyre House   70
Jefferson Avenue Townhouses   71
Wright Carriage House   71
Lowenstein House   72
Bradford-Maydwell House   75
Patton House   76

■ GREENLAW   77
- Porter-Leath Children's Center   78
- Harris Memorial Methodist Church   79
- George C. Love House   80
- Artesian Water Pumping Station   82
- Burkle House   83

■ VANCE-PONTOTOC   84

■ ADDITIONAL MEMPHIS ARCHITECTURE   85
- Elmwood Cemetery   86
- Coward Place   88
- Annesdale   90
- Ashlar Hall   94
- Rozelle House   95
- Rayner House   96
- Elam House   98
- Buntyn-Ramsay House   100
- Maxwelton (Sneed-Ewell House)   102
- Captain Harris House   103
- Richards House   104
- Tennessee Brewery   106
- Marine Hospital   108

SHELBY COUNTY   109
Seven Hills Plantation   110
■ RALEIGH   112
Goodwinslow   112
Graham House   115
■ BARTLETT   116
Glendale   117
Blackwell House   118
Smith-McKenzie House   119
Yates-Marr House   120
Gotten House   121
■ Davies Manor   122
Griffin House   124
Cedar Hall   125
■ CORDOVA   128
Ecklin House   129
Mt. Airy   130
■ ARLINGTON   132
Tall Cedar Cottage   132
Will-Hugh   132
Marley House   133
Shelton House   133
Green Gables   134
Bone House   135
Herron House   135
■ GERMANTOWN   136
Germantown Presbyterian
  Church   138
Germantown Baptist Church   140
Shepherd-Arthur House   141
Williams House   142
Whitlow House   143
Sullivan House   143
Woodlawn   144
Richwood   146

Mosby-Bennett House   148
■ COLLIERVILLE   150
DeLoach House   152
Virginius Leake House   154
Davis-Porter House   156
Fleming Place   158
Stratton-Owen Place   160
Collierville Presbyterian Church   162
Nolley House   163
Humphreys House   163
St. Andrew's Episcopal Church   164
■ WHITEHAVEN   166
Hale House   166
Hilderbrand House   167

AFTERWORD   168
ARCHITECTURAL
  GLOSSARY   169
CREDITS   174
BIBLIOGRAPHY   176
NOTES   178
INDEX   183

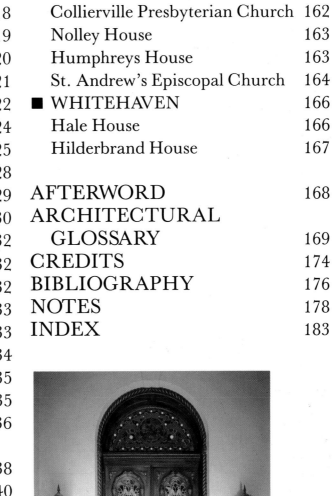

PREFACE

This book began in 1977 when members of Memphis Heritage came to the Junior League of Memphis asking for help with a project to photograph and document old buildings in the city. For two years volunteers, under the chairmanship of Susan Patton Robinson, worked with Memphis Heritage researching old buildings. Gradually the project grew, first into a proposed pamphlet, then into a book. The geographic limits grew, too, expanding from the city into the county under the chairmanship of Snowden Boyle Morgan and Mary Martin Malone. Over the five year span, more than forty League members have worked on the book. In 1982, under the chairmanship of Helen Scanling Hays and Ginny Muller Strubing, the book took its final form with Perre Magness as writer, Murray Riss as photographer and Towery Press as co-publisher with the Junior League of Memphis.

A word must be said on the final determination of buildings chosen. Our criteria were: buildings erected before 1900, still standing, without too much alteration to the facade. Obviously not all the nineteenth century buildings still standing in Shelby County could be included, so consideration was given to the style of the building, its association with people or events in local history, its present appearance and condition, and the availability of information.

In choosing the buildings to be included we have relied on much help and advice from the Memphis Landmarks Commission and several county historians: Mrs. Frances Herring in Arlington, Mrs. Elva Bledsoe in Bartlett, Mrs. Clarene Russell in Collierville, Mrs. Betty Hughes in Germantown, Mrs. Eleanor Hughes in Memphis, and Mrs. Mary Chapman in Raleigh.

We particularly wish to thank:

Jim Johnson and the staff of the Memphis Room at the Memphis and Shelby County Public Library,

Peggy Jemison and Emily Ruch for training volunteers,

Dr. Charles Crawford of Memphis State University for checking the manuscript,

Walk Jones, III, for checking the architectural glossary,

and all those people who graciously opened their homes, their scrapbooks and their memories to us. ∎

Helen Hays and Ginny Strubing
Co-Chairmen

JUNIOR LEAGUE COMMITTEE

Buff Adams	*Harriett Flinn*	*Linda May*	*Ann Styron*
Deby Baker	*Mary-Ann Gano*	*Maryan Mercer*	*Mary G. Sullivan*
Pam Bryce	*Marietta Haaga*	*Anne Miller*	*Valerie Thompson*
Stephanie Cannon	*Ann Hawkins*	*Snow Morgan*	*Ainslie Todd*
Nancy Chase	*Jessica Heckle*	*Robin Powell*	*Jennifer Treadwell*
Penny Dart	*Mary Hewes*	*Susan P. Robinson*	*Sally Treadwell*
Mary O. Davis	*Marilyn Hubbard*	*Beanie Self*	*Louise Tual*
Mary Deibel	*Liza Kirk*	*Lou Slater*	*Cathy Turner*
Blanche Deaderick	*Mary Malone*	*Linda G. Smith*	*Jenni Turner*
Becky Deupree	*Martha McKellar*	*Robbie Smith*	*Carol Watson*
Beth Elzemeyer	*Linda Kay McCloy*	*Elise Stratton*	*Nora Witmer*
			Lucy Woodson

INTRODUCTION

The earliest man-made structures to be recorded on the Fourth Chickasaw Bluff showed the adaptation to natural conditions which characterizes good architecture. Marquette and Joliet, on their trip down the Mississippi River in 1673, paused at the site of future Memphis long enough to comment on the Indians there, whom they called Monsoupeleas. The Indians lounged on elevated wooden platforms or grids, canopied in skins, with smudge fires underneath to drive off the mosquitoes. Generations of later Bluff residents might well have envied the Indians this solution to a vexing problem.

Indians, animals and insects had long shared the lands of western Tennessee and northern Mississippi. By about 800 A.D. the Indians were living in settled communities stretching for about forty miles southward along the Mississippi from the mouth of the Wolf River. By the time the first European travellers entered the area in the sixteenth century, the Chickasaws were the dominant tribe and called their group of towns "Quiz Quiz."

The first Europeans were Spaniards under the leadership of Hernando DeSoto, exploring the area in the name of the Spanish crown in 1541. Somewhere in the general vicinity of Memphis, DeSoto's tattered army built rafts and crossed the Mississippi. The main thing DeSoto did (besides giving his name to a modern bridge) was to provide historians with a source of endless debate about exactly where he first encountered the river.

More than a hundred years passed before white men appeared again. This time they were French and coming from the north: a Jesuit, Jacques Marquette, and a fur trader, Louis Joliet, who were descending the Mississippi in 1673 in the name of those two great themes of exploration: religion and commerce. The Indians that Joliet and Marquette found on the bluff had, besides mosquito repellent, powder, knives and beads, proving that the culture of Europe was creeping into the interior of North America. Another Frenchman, LaSalle, stopped at the bluff nine years later. Traffic was definitely picking up.

By the 1730s, when travel along the Mississippi had increased, the Chickasaw tribe was definitely in control. The four bluffs, located within a space of sixty miles along the eastern bank of the river, were recog-

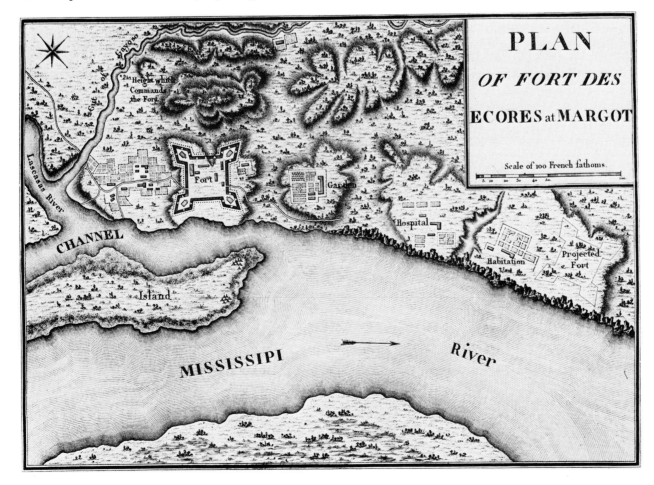

AT LEFT:
The earliest record of European architecture in Tennessee: the plan of San Fernando de las Barrancas, 1796.

nized for their strategic importance. Located between the Gulf of Mexico and the Ohio tributary, the high ground, safe from flooding, represented the key to controlling the middle Mississippi Valley and was a traditional site for Indian trade.

France, England and Spain all had their eyes on the interior of the continent. Missionaries, soldiers and traders began to travel the great waterway. The first to stop for long at the fourth bluff was Jean Baptiste LeMoyne, Sieur de Bienville, French governor of the Louisiana Territory. He arrived with a troop of soldiers in 1739, and built Fort Assumption, three fourths of a league below the mouth of the Wolf River (near the eastern end of the Memphis-Arkansas Bridge). But within a few months his mission had failed, the victim of disease, the Chickasaws, and European politics.

In 1763 a proclamation gave the land on the east bank of the Mississippi above the Yazoo River to the British and the land along the western bank to the Spanish. The Chickasaws, enemies of the French, were more receptive to British claims. But before the British could firmly establish their rights in the interior, they began to have problems with the colonists along the eastern seaboard. Only after the American Revolution did traders, scouts and settlers begin to make their way in any numbers across the Appalachians into the wilderness.

But the Spanish were still ambitious, and were glad to capitalize on the troubles of the British and the French, whose own revolution began in 1789. Despite the fact that land grants in the western part of what had been North Carolina were being issued as early as 1783, the Spanish, under Don Manuel Gayoso, arrived in May, 1795, to purchase land from the Chickasaws and to erect a fort called San Fernando de las Barrancas (Saint Ferdinand of the Bluffs) at a location near the foot of present-day Auction Street.

This is the first example of European architecture of which we have a record. A detailed plan, dated 1796, shows a fortification, squatters' huts, a fairly elaborate formal garden, a hospital and other dependencies, and a "habitation." The fort was about two hundred feet long on each side with bastions extending it on the corners. Around the fortification developed trading posts and more squatters' huts.

Spanish occupation lasted less than two years. In 1797, one year after Tennessee became a state, the garrison withdrew across the river to Esperanza (Hopefield), leaving behind the few settlers and traders who had clustered around the fort. In July, 1797, these stragglers welcomed American troops under Captain Isaac Guion, who established Fort Adams. Soon a more permanent settlement, Fort Pickering, named for the Secretary of State, Timothy Pickering, was built further south, near the site of former Fort Assumption and present-day DeSoto Park. Its commandants included Captain Zebulon Pike, whose son gave his name to Pike's Peak, and young Lieutenant Zachary Taylor, future Mexican War hero and president of the United States.

The American presence assured the arrival of more settlers, including Paddy Meagher of Bell Tavern fame, and Isaac Rawlings (who was to become the second mayor of Memphis) who were living on the bluff by 1814. But life was harsh and could barely be called civilization.

Enter the real estate developers. From the very beginnings they have played an inordinately large role in the life of the Memphis area. On October 23, 1783, the legislature of North Carolina opened the land around Memphis for purchase. The fact that it was Chickasaw land was a minor annoyance. On that opening day John Rice purchased, for $2,500, five thousand acres fronting on the Mississippi at the mouth of the Wolf River, and John Ramsey purchased five thousand acres immediately to the south of the Rice grant.

A rough survey was made in 1786, but Rice was killed by Indians in 1791, and his brother sold the claim to John Overton for five hundred dollars. Overton had an agreement with Andrew Jackson about land speculation, and for the sum of one hundred dollars Jackson became a partner. In 1797, Jackson sold one-half of his share to two Winchester brothers, Stephan and Richard, who in turn passed their portion to their brother James.

Overton, Jackson and Winchester thus were the first proprietors of Memphis; at the turn of the century they owned a tract of wilderness with the advantage of a strategic location. All three lived comfortably in Middle Tennessee, where their homes were architectural showpieces. Overton, a judge, built Traveller's Rest at Nashville in 1799. James Winchester, a general in the army, built Cragfont near Gallatin in 1802. Andrew Jackson was busy fighting Indians in Florida and the British at New Orleans and didn't get around to giving the Hermitage near Nashville its present form till 1831. All three men enjoyed the gracious comforts of civilization a far piece from their rugged frontier holdings.

But what about the Chickasaws? The land on the bluff was theirs, but like the more recent claimants, they preferred to live someplace else. Their main settlements were near present-day Tupelo, one hundred miles away in northeast Mississippi, but for generations they had used the bluff and surroundings for hunting grounds, for harassing the French and Spanish, and for access to river trade and travel. Their claim to the land had to be settled. In 1818 President Monroe appointed General Andrew Jackson and Isaac Shelby, a Revolutionary war soldier who became governor of Kentucky, to negotiate a treaty with the Indians.

What happened next has occasioned as much debate among historians as the whereabouts of DeSoto and his men. In 1818 Jackson and Shelby negotiated the Chickasaw Cession, or Western Purchase. On October

19 the treaty was signed. The Indians ceded over six million acres of West Tennessee land for fifteen annual payments of $20,000 each plus a few minor considerations. Thus the lands were sold for less than five cents an acre. Whether their part was honorable, despicable or merely expedient, Jackson and Shelby assured once and for all that West Tennessee was part of the United States.

Future settlers might well have wondered why so many of the previous owners of the area preferred to live elsewhere, but the prospect of new land was enticing. To be ready for the buyers, General Winchester

The first setback to Overton's town on the bluff came in 1824, when a state commission chose a site on the Wolf River at Sanderlin's Bluff, nearer the center of the county, to be the county seat. This was the first but not the last time Memphis met resistance in the state legislature. The town of Raleigh was immediately laid out as the site for the courts, growing to a peak in about 1836. But the location of Memphis again played a part, and the harbor for the ever-increasing flatboat traffic along the Mississippi insured its growth. For a time its most serious rival was the town of Randolph, a community forty-two miles upstream

AT RIGHT:
An 1828 sketch of the Bluff by a French artist, LeSueur.

sent his son, Marcus, to be the on-site representative of the proprietors. William Lawrence drew a survey plan, and on May 1, 1819, Overton, Winchester and Lawrence laid out the town with lots for sale and lots set aside for public use. General Winchester chose the name Memphis from the corrupted Greek name, meaning "Good Abode," of the city on the Nile in Egypt, probably inspired by the Napoleanic campaigns in Egypt. The land boom was on.

But business was slow at first. John Overton was the most eager promoter of the investment, placing ads in newspapers around the country. In November of 1819, the Tennessee legislature created Shelby County, and Overton immediately began campaigning for Memphis to be named the county seat, knowing that legal affairs would attract other business. The quarterly court first met in Memphis in May, 1820, but lot sales were slow.

Even before the Chickasaw Cession, a few settlers had made their way into the county, and there were farmers clearing land as well as traders clustering around the forts. Big Creek, near the present-day town of Millington, and Egypt, a few miles south, were two of the earliest settlements in Shelby County.

on the second Chickasaw bluff, near the mouth of the Hatchie River. Until 1838 Randolph was a serious contender for the river trade.

Visitors to Memphis commented on the rough character of the settlement, but one came with a vision of the future and made plans to stay. In 1825, Frances Wright, a rich Scots spinster and protegee of LaFayette, arrived looking for a location for her idea of Utopia. She bought 2000 acres of land up the Wolf River from Raleigh, near what is today Shelby Farms at Germantown. Here she planned her ideal community and called it "Nashoba," the Chickasaw word for wolf. Her plan was to buy slaves, educate them for self-sufficiency in an atmosphere where blacks and whites lived together in harmony, then set them free. Her dream lasted less than five years. Fanny Wright freed her slaves and sent them to Haiti, and then moved on to Robert Owen's New Harmony, advocating equality for blacks and women for the rest of her life.

Settlement and progress continued apace. Families from North Carolina formed a community around Cordova in the 1830s, and families from Virginia settled nearby. A Methodist circuit rider was making regular stops in Memphis by 1826. By 1832 a log meeting house had been erected in Court Square and by 1836 Eugene Magevney was using the building on weekdays as a school house. In 1826 the first newspaper appeared, and in 1840 the *Appeal* began publication which continues today. By 1840, too, all denominations of religion were represented on the bluff. Marcus Winchester had been elected the first mayor in 1827, to be succeeded by Isaac Rawlings in 1829.

But in 1828 there was a portent of evil to come: the first yellow fever epidemic occurred. The same year a flood changed the river front, leaving a sandbar along the public landing and reminding the settlers of the power of the Mississippi.

Cotton was beginning its rise to King. In 1825 three hundred bales were traded in Memphis; within fifteen years the number had grown to 35,000 bales. With the growth of the cotton market came a corresponding growth in the number of slaves needed to grow it. In the frontier days a strong sentiment existed for the freeing of slaves, but as the plantation economy became more dependent upon their labor, repression grew and the seeds of tragedy were sown.

The flatboat traffic along the Mississippi gave the settlement its first impetus to growth, but also brought a rough and ready element to the town. Memphis had a natural landing: an eddy at the mouth of Gayoso Bayou made it easy for flatboats to steer into Catfish Bay. Around the harbor a shanty town, constructed with the lumber from the flatboats, grew up and gained the name of Pinch, or Pinchgut, for the poor people who lived there. In retaliation for the name, the inhabitants of Pinch called the area to the south Sodom, and a rivalry grew between the two for the river landing. An all-out flatboat war occured in 1841 when Mayor Spickernagle was elected on a "reform" ticket, and began to enforce landing fees for the unruly flatboatmen.

The town of Memphis had other rivals in South Memphis and Ft. Pickering. John C. McLemore, married to a niece of Andrew Jackson, had acquired land in the Ft. Pickering area. He was an early believer in the promise of the railroads and sold lots in the Ft. Pickering area in an attempt to get the Memphis and LaGrange Railroad to make that its terminus. In the financial panic of 1837 the railroad almost went under, and by 1841 the line only ran east as far as Colonel Eppy White's Station.

South Memphis had been largely developed by Robertson Topp south of today's Union Avenue, and had its moment of glory when it secured a steamboat landing for the boats that were increasingly replacing flatboats. Businesses began to

spring up on the streets around Topp's grand Gayoso Hotel, built in 1844 on Front between McCall and Gayoso, and South Memphis was incorporated as a separate town in 1846. Finally in 1850 the rivalry was settled when Memphis absorbed South Memphis.

These were the boom years. The markets for cotton and other goods were growing. The railroads finally linked the Mississippi and the Atlantic with the completion of the Memphis and Charleston line in 1857. The population was increasing with immigrants from Ireland and Germany; between 1840 and 1845 the number of inhabitants doubled, and during the next five years it doubled again. In 1856 the first new addition to the original plan was opened as the Greenlaw brothers developed their subdivision north of Gayoso Bayou.

From the first log huts around the forts and the board shanties around the flatboat landings, the architecture of Memphis became more sophisticated. Frontier log houses like Davies Manor and the Elam Homestead were built simultaneously with plantation-style Greek Revival houses like the Pillow-McIntyre house in Memphis, Cedar Hall and the Ecklin House in the county. Eugene Magevney's simple clapboard cottage and the Italianate splendor of Annesdale are only separated by eighteen years. Memphis was a town in a hurry; there was no time to develop an indigenous style. Memphis was tied to St. Louis and New Orleans as Nashville and Middle Tennessee were tied to Virginia and the eastern seaboard. And Memphis had a large share of the frontier spirit in its make-up.

Where plantation-style homes were built by the prosperous citizens of the county, the aristocracy of Memphis was built on commerce, railroads and land speculation rather than on an agrarian tradition. Therefore, when the cotton factors and wholesale grocers who made up the top of Memphis society built their houses, they chose showy French and Italianate Victorian, like the mansions along Adams Avenue,

AT RIGHT:
After the Civil War Napolean Hill prospered as a cotton factor and banker, and built this Victorian extravaganza at Third and Madison, where the Sterick Building stands today.

rather than the more restrained Greek Revival style chosen by their neighbors in the county and in north Mississippi.

Carpenters, pioneers and slaves had built the first houses in the new territory, but soon architects appeared. In 1845, one William Crane advertised in the *Appeal* that his services could save a potential homeowner money: "A few dollars paid in the commencement, to an architect who understands his profession, will save hundreds in the end." James B. Cook arrived in Memphis in 1857; he had studied architecture and engineering in England, and had worked on the Crystal Palace in London. The technical skills that he brought to the frontier were a far cry from the simple carpentry of the log construction of the Elam Homestead. Time passed quickly on the frontier, and Memphis was a crossroads.

The villages developing in rural Shelby County were very different from the rough and ready town on the river. Throughout the 1840s and 1850s settlers came to farm the rich West Tennessee soil, and small communities grew around a stage stop or a post office. Collierville was the largest with two hundred and fifty residents in the 1850s. Wythe Depot, Marysville, and Morning Sun were others. The churches, schools and general stores that grew up in the midst of plantations and farms were a far cry from the elegant hostelries (like the Gayoso House) that catered to rich cotton factors or the taverns that served riverboat men that were growing up in Memphis.

As the Civil War approached, Memphis was a border city in a border state, between north and south, on the edge of the old east and the new west. River trade came from both St. Louis and New Orleans. The economy was dependent on the cotton trade with its slave base, but there had been a large influx of German and Irish immigrants.

In 1860 the citizens of Memphis had voted eight to one in favor of pro-Union candidates, but by the next year the tide had turned. On April 2, 1861, Memphis voted to join the Confederacy. Then Fort Sumpter in South Carolina fell and the war was on.

Shelby Countians volunteered for the Confederate Army in droves, forming troops called the Wigfall Grays in Collierville, the Emerald Guards, the Bluff City Grays, the Crockett Rangers, the Jeff Davis Invincibles, the Garibaldi Guards and the Harris Zouaves. Although the strategic importance of Memphis as a crossroads of rail and river was obvious, the city's defenses were few. Business was better than ever, with frantic movement of goods and people. The city's foundaries and factories ran at full tilt.

In April of 1862 the war came closer. Confederate-fortified Island 10 above Memphis fell to the Union, and the battles of Shiloh and Corinth to the east gave the Northern troops control of the railroads and opened the approaches to Memphis to the Union on both sides. In fear of seizure, Memphians burned 300,000 bales of cotton on the waterfront.

Shortly after dawn on June 6, 1862, the Union fleet steamed into sight around a bend in the river with five ironclads, each with thirteen heavy cannons, and two Ellet rams, a new untried fast boat whose job was to sink enemy ships. Spectators lined the bluff, a magnificent ringside seat from which to see the Yankees vanquished.

But within an hour and a half the Confederate ships were destroyed. By seven a.m. it was over. Memphis was a conquered city and the Mississippi was open to the Yankees all the way to Vicksburg. The commander of the Union forces landed a party and marched them to the post office on the corner of Third and Jefferson, where the Stars and Stripes was raised. The mayor, John Park, replied, "That as the civil authorities have no means of defense , by the force of circumstances the city is in your hands."

The federal occupation meant that Memphis was spared the physical destruction that occured in Collierville when Union soldiers burned the town. Memphis was a Federal island in a sea of Confederates. General U. S. Grant was the commander in July, 1862, with his headquarters in the Hunt home on Beale Street. At least ten generals were in command over Memphis, including General William Tecumseh Sherman, whose harshness in banishing disloyal families and seizing their property was legendary. The Irving Block on Court Square was an infamous prison.

But the citizens waged a private war. Memphis became a center of contraband activities. Weapons, gold and cotton continued to pass through Memphis. By 1863 the population had doubled — Negroes from the surrounding agricultural counties poured in, and so did Yankee speculators, soldiers and businessmen. The raids of General Nathan Bedford Forrest and his cavalry were famous, culminating in the famous raid of August 21, 1864, when a Union general fled in his nightshirt. The raids proved the vulnerability of Memphis.

The Civil War gave rise to a body of folklore much loved by Southerners. Every antebellum house in Memphis has its tale of buried silver. If General Grant had stopped at every house he is reported to have visited, he would have been a much longer time winning the war. (Similarly, Jefferson Davis, who lived in Memphis for a time after the war, is reported to have been entertained at so many houses that it is no wonder he had to move to Richmond in order to earn a living.)

Few Southern cities suffered so little physically as did Memphis during the Civil War. In fact, building continued, with the Union army even helping at the dedication of St. Mary's Roman Catholic Church. Although many individuals had been ruined by the war, trade had continued and the population had grown. But the city depended upon the surrounding countryside and in Mississippi, Arkansas and Tennessee, farms were ruined, buildings were destroyed, and railroads and levees were gone. Collierville had been burned by Union soldiers, and Germantown damaged.

The social order was destroyed. The black population of Memphis had increased from 3,000 in 1860 to 15,000 in 1870, and these new residents needed education, employment, and housing. The Freedman's Bureau attempted to deal with their needs but the numbers were staggering. Violence erupted in May, 1866, in a fight between 4,000 black soldiers awaiting release at Ft. Pickering and Irish policemen. After three days of violence, white troops sent in from Nashville restored order, but forty-four blacks and two whites had been killed and property damage was great. The next year the Ku Klux Klan made its terrifying appearance.

The change was economic, social and political. The South was used to a dominant role in national politics; her sons had been presidents, and controlled the courts and congress. Now, subservience was the role of the South.

With the end of slavery the plantation economy was in turmoil. A new labor system had to be devised, and the adjustment to the tenant farmer system was difficult. A new group in the social order, freedmen, had to be absorbed. As early as 1851 a free black had owned land on Beale Street, but the large numbers of blacks pouring in from the farms had nothing. Organizations — benevolent and social orders — sprang up to take care of their needs.

At war's end roads, railroads and livestock were in a sorry state. Many white businessmen and farmers had been killed and others refused to sign the loyalty oath. Bitterness and political instability were legacies that lasted well into the next decades. In 1867 another yellow fever epidemic and a severe outbreak of cholera struck. Violence and lawlessness seemed the order of the day. Financial panics and repressive policies by Governor Brownlow added to Memphis' woes.

Slowly the city began to reconstruct itself. When Federal troops departed undoubtedly they were as glad to go as the citizens were to see them leave, for Memphis was decaying physically and fiscally. Sanitation was non-existent. Water came from cisterns often located close to privies, from shallow wells, or from the Wolf River. The streets were seas of mud; those which were paved were covered with a system of wooden paving blocks which were sinking and decaying in the ooze. Wagons bringing heavy loads of cotton mired up at every turn. The city government struggled with an increasing debt in an attempt to provide any services at all.

And worse was yet to come. In 1873 yellow fever struck again with 5,000 cases and 2,000 deaths. In 1878 17,600 cases and over 5,000 deaths were reported in Memphis; Bartlett reported twenty-three deaths; Collierville fifty-seven; Germantown, forty-five and Raleigh, eighteen. No one knew what caused the plagues. Filth, the water supply, the decaying pavements, "miasmas" from the swamps, the extreme

heat of summer — all were blamed, but no one yet suspected the mosquito.

Many citizens fled. Towns all around announced quarantines against freight and passengers from afflicted areas. Historian J. M. Keating, writing in 1888, described the exodus:

> Out by the country roads to the little hamlets, villages and plantations where many had been welcome guests in happier days, out by every possible conveyance, by hacks, by carriages, buggies, wagons, furniture vans and street drays; away by batteaux, by anything that could float upon the river, and by railroads, the trains on which, especially on the Louisville Road, were so packed as to make the trip to that city or Cincinnati, even to strong and hardy men, a positive torture every mile of the way. (p. 655)

Those brave souls who stayed to care for the afflicted are remembered as martyrs: Catholic priests; Episcopal nuns; a madam who turned her house of ill repute into a hospital; the Howard Association which had been organized in 1867 to provide care for paupers. The doctors were practically helpless. Refugee camps were set up, curfews and patrols were organized. Order broke down and violence broke out. Still the people died. In the middle of September, 1878, two hundred people a day were dying. The **Avalanche** wrote:

> Surely our cup of sorrows must be full. Black as the dead list is today in our city, it fails to represent all those ready for burial yesterday. The county undertaker has four furniture wagons busy all day. Upon each the coffins were piled as high as safety from falling would permit. These four great vehicles, doing the wholesale burying business, failed to take to the potters field all of the indigent dead. At the time the officer made his report, sixty bodies were awaiting interment.
>
> *Quoted by Quinn, p. 195*

On October 18, 1878, a killing frost came. Prayers of thanksgiving were offered and on the twenty-ninth the epidemic was declared at an end. The number of tombstones in Elmwood Cemetary dating from the plague years are mute testimony to the loss.

The refugees who returned found a broken city. Memphis was at the lowest ebb in its fortunes. Real estate values had collapsed, the population had shrunk, public services were in disarray, and municipal indebtedness had compounded. In 1870 Memphis had been larger than Atlanta or Nashville; in 1880 it was smaller. The mosquito had done what the war had not.

In January, 1879, the city ceased to exist as a cor-

porate entity. The political leadership asked the state legislature to take the charter, and that strange creature, the Taxing District, under the control of the state, was established until the debts were paid. That summer another epidemic occurred, less violent but still frightening. Memphis had been the worst hit of all the Mississippi Valley towns in 1878, and the eyes of the nation were focused here. The National Board of Health and various citizens' committees set about to take strong measures.

Dr. D. T. Porter, first president of the Taxing District (a post akin to mayor), and his successor David Park Hadden, presided over the clean-up. A new sewage system was begun and fifty-two miles of Waring sewers were laid in twenty years. The wooden Nicholson block pavements were replaced by hard surface pavements. A Board of Health started a house-to-house census by sanitary police, meat and milk inspections, garbage service and other measures. In 1887 the first drilling of an artesian well made a safe public water supply possible. The city charter was restored in 1893.

From the ruins a new city grew. A large part of the German and Irish population had gone, taking with them the potential for a more cosmopolitan city. Cotton was still King, but hardwood had also begun to be a factor in the economy. Telephones and electricity appeared in the 1880s. The railroads continued to grow, and in 1892 the railroad bridge across the Mississippi was built. It was the first bridge to be built below St. Louis and it extended trade to the West. Fifty thousand people watched the first train cross; many attended a celebration at the Fontaine home. Rail-

roads were changing the face of the county; settlements consolidated along the railroad routes and became towns in the 1870s and 1880s.

People, both black and white, moved into Memphis from the surrounding countryside. The legend of Beale Street began to take shape; its saloons, pool halls, theaters, pawnshops, gambling dens and stores echoed to the music that was to make it famous. It was becoming "the Main Street of Negro America."

The last two decades of the nineteenth century were a time of building. New technologies showed in the architecture: cast iron could imitate cheaply what stone work had done; the power-driven jigsaw made flights of decorative fancy in wood possible. New building materials could be used because of improved transportation; those two constants of every ante-bellum house, "hand-hewn logs" and "bricks fired on the place," gave way to granite and limestone. Even a skyscraper could be built, to the wonder of the citizenry.

Prosperity showed in the building of the homes along Adams, Beale and Vance Avenues. Architectural styles usually come down to us through public buildings and the homes of the rich, which are built to last. But Shelby County has a treasure trove of middle class housing left — in Greenlaw and in the towns of Arlington, Bartlett and Germantown. While ostentation was the rule in the silk-stocking districts of Memphis, comfort was the rule in the county.

In 1899 Memphis again annexed its suburbs, quadrupling its size and changing its axis from north-south to east-west. With a population of just over 100,000 and growing, Memphis stood ready to greet the new century. ∎

1541 DeSoto claims the region for Spain; crosses the Mississippi . . . somewhere.

1673 Joliet and Marquette stop at the Fourth Chickasaw Bluff on their trip down the Mississippi.

1682 LaSalle visits the Bluff and claims it for France.

1739 Bienville builds Fort Assumption near eastern end of today's three bridges.

1763 End of French and Indian War gives England claim to Bluff.

1783 Treaty of Paris gives new United States claim to Bluff. John Rice and John Ramsey enter claims for 5,000 acres each.

1794-1796 John Overton and Andrew Jackson aquire Rice grant.

1795 Spanish build San Fernando de las Barrancas, a fort near today's Auction Square.

1796 Tennessee becomes sixteenth state.

1797 Americans build Fort Adams on site of San Fernando.

1798 Fort Pickering built two miles south of Fort Adams.

1818 Chickasaw Cession. Andrew Jackson and Isaac Shelby negotiate sale of over six million acres for fifteen annual payments of $20,000.

1819 William Lawrence and Marcus Winchester survey the Bluff. Memphis is laid out.

1820s First mail service. Settlement at Big Creek north of Memphis.

1824 Sanderlin's Bluff chosen as county seat. Raleigh laid out.

1826 Frances Wright organizes Nashoba colony near today's Germantown. First organized religion appears upon the bluff in the form of a Methodist circuit rider.

1826 Memphis chartered. Marcus Winchester first mayor.

1834 First school on Court Square organized by Eugene Magevney. Treaty with Chickasaw Nation cedes northern Mississippi.

1835 Memphis-LaGrange Railroad chartered. Settlements around Morning Sun (near Cordova).

1841 Germantown incorporated.

1842 Flatboat war in Memphis. Railroad reaches to White's Station.

1846 South Memphis incorporated.

1849 Memphis and South Memphis merge.

1850s Memphis fastest growing city in United States, and largest inland cotton market.

1855 Memphis and Charleston Railroad reaches Germantown and Collierville.

1856 Memphis and Ohio Railroad reaches Union Depot (Bartlett), Bond's Station (Ellendale), Brunswick, Wythe Depot (Arlington). Greenlaw subdivision laid out.

1857 "Wedding of the Waters" — Atlantic and Mississippi River joined by rail.

1861 Secession and Civil War.

1862 Federal occupation of Memphis. Germantown raided.

1863 Battle of Collierville. Collierville destroyed.

1865 Civil War ends.

1866 Race riot in Memphis. Bartlett incorporated.

1867 Third yellow fever epidemic.

1870 Memphis annexes Greenlaw, Chelsea, Ft. Pickering. Collierville incorporated.

1872 Haysville laid out around Wythe Depot (Arlington).

1873 Fourth yellow fever epidemic. Memphis Cotton Exchange established.

1877 End of Reconstruction.

1878 Fifth and deadliest yellow fever epidemic.

1879 City Charter surrendered, Memphis becomes Taxing District. Still another siege of yellow fever.

1883 Haysville name changed to Arlington.

1887 Artesian water discovered in Memphis.

1891 Raleigh Springs developed as resort.

1893 Charter of Memphis restored.

1899 Memphis annexes suburbs and quadruples size.

MEMPHIS

"Court Square in Summer"

To see Memphis in a "nut shell," the Northern tourist should enter that beautiful city "reservation" known as Court Square. From this impaled enclosure, the visitor can enjoy the beauties of both country and city life. On the green, daisy-bedecked sward, shaded by miniature forests of lilac, cypress, myrtle and cedar trees, moistened by the spray of its marble fountain, might be seen artistic flower beds, circumscribed by mimic walls of pinks, geraniums, violets and heliotropes . . . . But to the Northern tourist there is nothing half so enchanting as the climatic mocking bird, poised on some leafy bough of the Southern native and imcomparably fragrant "Magnolia."

— *Quinn, Heroes and Heroines of Memphis, 1887*

Court Square

The history of Court Square begins in 1819, when the first surveyors envisioned the new town on the fourth Chickasaw Bluff. The original proprietors of Memphis, General Andrew Jackson, Judge John Overton and General James Winchester, had acquired the land from the heirs of one John Rice in the 1790s, but only after the conclusion of a treaty with the Chickasaws did they have a town survey made. James Winchester's son Marcus and surveyor William Lawrence completed their survey by May 22, 1819, and gave the town the name of Memphis.

"For a day when city planning had not been thought of west of the Alleghenies, the village was excellently laid out — at least on paper," wrote historian Gerald Capers. Streets ran to the points of the compass, a promenade would extend along the river front, and four public squares, named for their purposes — Auction, Court, Exchange, and Market — were set aside for public use.

The nearly two acres reserved for the building of a court house between Main and Second Streets had a hard time living up to its name. To Overton's surprise the county seat of Shelby County was fixed at Sanderlin's Bluff on the Wolf River, there the town of Raleigh was laid out, and there the courts were to convene.

Deprived of its use as a site for a court house, the tract was the subject of litigation as to what public purpose it should fill. In 1834 (and again in 1903) the Tennessee Supreme Court ruled that the city was free to use the land as it pleased.

A building constructed of black gum logs was erected in the square and used as a school house, with Eugene Magevney as schoolmaster. The first church services were held in the log cabin, and continued to be held there, as late as 1838.

By 1849 the Square was serving its purpose as a public park, an early urban oasis, and citizens were taking an interest in the wildlife. A resident of Bolivar, Tennessee, donated two gray squirrels to the city in the hope that they would "add to the animation of the Square."

On May 18, 1858, the eagle living in Court Square was found dead, victim of another resident, a racoon. Angry citizens hunted down the predator and destroyed him, with the result that Colonel Finnie, C.M. Fackler, and Robert Baker were fined five dollars each for shooting within the city limits.

In 1894 the Goodman brothers donated two fine foxes to be placed in the Square. Into the next century the wildlife was a subject of civic pride. By 1929 Judge James H. Malone felt it necessary to start a subscription list for money to provide daily meals for the squirrels and pigeons, but later the Park Commission took over this responsibility. Perhaps they were too well fed, because in 1931 citizens were looking for a solution to the squirrel problem. Men carrying long fishing poles with cheese cloth sacks attached stalked the squirrels at night and transferred them to Overton Park.

A bust of Andrew Jackson by sculptor Nelson Swa-

zey was given to the city by Joel Parrish and erected in Court Square in 1857. The words "Our Federal Union: it must be preserved" were engraved on the base. During the Civil War the words enraged some Confederate soldiers, who tried to erase them. Only in 1908 were the words put back. The bust was removed to the Court House in 1921.

Mrs. Elizabeth Meriwether, in her *Recollections of Ninety-Two Years,* recalls the horror of the Irving Block, an office building on Second Street that General Sherman had converted into a prison from 1862 to 1865. From its windows, Confederate prisoners could gaze upon Court Square's trees and squirrels. At the close of the war about twelve hundred soldiers and one hundred citizens were incarcerated there. The threat of being sent to the Irving Block

hung over families of Confederate soldiers throughout the war.

For many years Court Square was the scene of public welcomes and farewells. Memphis soldiers marched past its reviewing stands on the way to four wars: the Mexican, Civil, Spanish-American and First World Wars. Every important visitor was welcomed there — Presidents Cleveland, Harrison and McKinley, Grand Duke Alexis of Russia, Davy Crockett, and Sam Houston.

The fountain and statue which are the symbol of Court Square today were erected under the supervision of architect James B. Cook for the United States Centennial Celebration and dedicated on May 28, 1876, before a crowd of 5,000 people. Fifty public spirited citizens had each donated $1,000 to erect the

ABOVE:
The Hebe Fountain in Court Square was erected by a group of public spirited citizens for the United States Centennial in 1876.

fountain, topped by a replica of a statue of Hebe, cup-bearer to the gods, the original of which is in Leningrad. Poor Hebe had been toppled by high winds and denounced (in 1932) by members of the Artists Guild as junk. People have wanted to sell her for scrap metal or to put more clothes on her. But she has remained serene. In 1947 it cost $1,750 to replace Hebe, and $11,050 to repair the fountain. By 1980 the cost of renovation had risen to $80,000.

In 1885 a young boy fell into the fountain and drowned, but that tragedy hasn't been repeated. In the 1950s catfish were put into the fountain, but that was a short-lived experiment, as people caught them and took them home for dinner.

A public drinking fountain with water pumped from the Wolf River was a feature of Court Square in the 1870s. Generous citizens were called upon to replace the drinking cups, which kept disappearing. There was other vandalism in the park. During concerts young boys would tie knots and loops in the long grasses. When dancers tried to skip about, they often became entangled and fell. The newspaper scolded the naughty boys and said the practice must come to a halt.

A popcorn stand, a Bible in a glass case with one page turned every day, colored lights in the fountain, a nativity scene — all have played their part in Court Square. In 1900 a brass Spanish cannon, cast in Seville in 1795, was placed in the Square, but its 3,600 pounds were sold for scrap metal during World War II. Today the Mid-America Mall borders Court Square on the west, and its stages are the scene for performances, festivals and celebrations.

How dull downtown Memphis would be if there were a courthouse instead of the greenspace of Court Square.

∎

Dr. D.T. Porter Building

1895

When the first skyscraper south of the Ohio was built in Memphis in 1895, it quickly became a tourist attraction. People came by train, by boat and by streetcar to pay ten cents to ride the elevator to the eleventh floor, go to the observation deck, and admire the marvelous view. The building superintendent described it to the *Press-Scimitar*: "Curiosity drew most of them here but some of them lost their nerve and wouldn't ride the elevator. Some of them were so frightened that after they rode to the top floor they'd get off and walk down." Trips were free until sundown, when the fare was a dime. Those brave enough to make it to the top were treated to music on the roof garden, with liquors and food offered in the rooftop nightclub.

Noted architect Edward Culliatt Jones, in one of his last commissions, designed the building at 10 North Main for the Continental Bank. The bank lobby had red marble wainscoting, Corinthian columns, ornate ceiling beams and a mosaic tile floor. But the bank failed in 1898, and the building was sold for $175,000 to the Porter family, who named it as a memorial to Dr. D.T. Porter.

David Tinsley Porter, a druggist turned business-man, was the first president of the Taxing District of Shelby County in 1878 after the city lost its charter. The city was burdened by debts and reduced to its lowest point by the devastation of the population by the yellow fever epidemics. The city charter was revoked by the state legislature, leaving the residents with little control over public affairs. Dr. Porter became president of the taxing district, equivalent to mayor.

Porter's direct methods in dealing with the crisis, improving sanitation and establishing a permanent Board of Health, did much to contribute to the rebirth of the city and the restoration of the charter in 1893. It is fitting that his name should be on the building which was a symbol of the vigor of the Gay Nineties in Memphis.

Architecturally, the building is a delight. The first two stories are Alabama limestone; the balance is granite, brick and terra cotta, with varied arches, ornamental lintels and carved cornices. The heavy cornice above the fifth floor corresponded with the height of the neighboring buildings at the time, but the east and south sides are blank because Jones thought the building was but the first of many tall ones.

The building was advertised as twelve stories: a basement, eleven full floors and a penthouse. It was said to be virtually fireproof because of its steel skeleton. Floors are still the original oak, corridors are tile floored and marble wainscoted. It had the latest in hot water heating — the highest building in the world to be heated by hot water.

It is now being converted from offices to residential space. The new tenants can still enjoy the elevator ride to a view of the city.

∎

Tennessee Club

1890

The eclectic mix of architectural elements in the building at the northeast corner of Court Square and Second Street attracts the eye of any visitor to downtown. Built for the Tennessee Club in 1890 by a Columbus, Ohio, architect named Edward Terrell, it now houses a law firm.

According to newspaper reports of the time, Mr. Terrell had a vision of the design in which everything was circular or curvilinear. Some undoubtedly considered it a nightmare. Windows, the corner tower, roof shapes and even interior spaces were in "forms as round as the Pantheon in Rome," the architect said. It was erected at a cost of $44,096 of rock-faced coursed ashlar sandstone and mortar in a distinctive red color. The use of semi-circular arches is typically Victorian Romanesque, but a Moorish influence can be seen in the bulbous dome, horseshoe arches, and stylized geometric and floral ornaments.

The south, or Court Square, facade has three sections. The center is a three-story rectangular plane originally planned with two sets of balconies "for watching parades or whatever was passing by" above the entrance. To the west is a wide rectangular section with a round opening on the third floor. On the east is a round corner tower.

The east, or Second Street, facade also has recessed sections and irregular window treatment. Over all is a bulbous dome with long windows with horseshoe arched tops.

The Tennessee Club was chartered in 1875 to establish a library and art gallery, foster debates in scientific research, and act as a social club. One can guess which of these purposes was given precedence. The men's grill in the basement had two tables, one reserved for "philosophers of the bar and business," the other for lumbermen who were solving "weighty" problems. Presidents Grant, Taft and Theodore Roosevelt were entertained by the club. The *Commercial Appeal* said of its membership in 1931, "To have free access to it, to be of the company that gathers there daily for lunch, bridge, or to loaf and read, is to have 'arrived' in Memphis."

Famous Tennessee Club Chicken

6	half breasts of chicken
6	tablespoons flour
6	tablespoons shortening
6	slices country ham
6	tablespoons ham fat
4	tablespoons butter
3	tablespoons flour
2	cups milk
$1/2$	cup sherry
6	toast circles
12	broiled fresh mushrooms

Carefully remove skin and bones from chicken breasts; ask butcher to cut breasts leaving wing bone to first joint. Dredge in flour, shake well to remove loose bits. Brown breasts in shortening in heavy bottomed frying pan, but do not cook tender. In a separate pan brown ham slices. Remove from pan, trim off fat and add fat back to pan with 2 tablespoons butter. Blend in flour, add milk and cook till thickened. Add sherry, stir well, season to taste. Place chicken pieces in sauce, cover tightly and cook in slow oven (300-325 degrees) till tender. The sauce should have the grace of proper consistency, too thick to run, too thin to clot, just thick enough to cling to the meat. On toast rounds, one to a plate, lay a slice of country ham trimmed to fit toast. Over the ham the chicken breast, wing tip up. Decorate each breast with 2 broiled mushroom caps. Pour over gravy. Place in oven till heated thoroughly. Serve immediately.

BELOW:
The Tennessee Club on Court Square, erected in 1890.

COTTON ROW

Cotton Row — the two short blocks of Front Street between Main and Gayoso — is the economic heart of Memphis. Well before the Civil War Memphis was a major cotton market, having out-stripped Vicksburg and Natchez, and beginning to rival New Orleans. Cotton came from the fertile delta lands and arrived in Memphis on wagons, by steamboats and barges, and, by the 1850s, by railroad. Even the setbacks of the Civil War and the yellow fever epidemics of the 1870s could not stop the growth of the cotton market. Cotton as a crop had moved west, and Memphis was the natural outlet, strengthened by the bridging of the Mississippi in the 1890s.

By the turn of the century Memphis was boasting of being the largest inland cotton market in the world. The emancipation of slaves and the breakup of the large plantations after the Civil War had resulted in a

new system of production, making the cotton factor all important. Not only did he advance credit to the planter, he supplied seed and goods for the plantation, and arranged the sale of the crop for a brokerage fee. He was banker, broker, grocer and supplier all in one. Cotton factors ruled Memphis in the '80s and '90s.

But the city was full of others connected to the trade: spinners' buyers, cotton classers, weighers, compress hands, ginners, binders, and clerks. Storage and compress facilities were built, and other businesses serving the cotton market — wholesale grocers and dry goods stores, seed merchants, hotels and bars — all grew up around Cotton Row.

In 1873 the Memphis Cotton Exchange was es-

tablished to bring order and information to the merchants and growers. Membership was limited to one hundred and seventy-five seats, creating a new power elite for the city. A thriving trade in cotton by-products grew up — cottonseed oil, crushed hulls for fertilizer and livestock feed — giving rise in 1881 to a commodities market known as the Memphis Merchants Exchange.

The rush season was October to January. Heavy bales were loaded onto mule wagons at the river landing, the drivers shouting as they urged their heavy loads up the bluff to Cotton Row. The streets in the neighborhood were (and still are) wider than most to allow the teams to zig zag up the steep grade. Long

ABOVE:
Cotton bales on the cobblestones of the Memphis Landing.

burlap "snakes" of cotton were piled on the sidewalk. Tufts of white fluff floated in the air.

The buildings of Cotton Row were constructed between 1848 and 1928 to suit their uses for the buying and selling of cotton. Built of brick, they had load-bearing walls and dirt basements and wide entrances for the bales. The interiors were anything but elegant, with offices on the first floor and storage rooms above. The top floors were equipped with skylights to light the classing rooms. Large interior spaces were designed for the handling of five hundred pound bales. The buildings were unpretentious and utilitarian, in sharp contrast to the flamboyance of other commercial buildings of this gaudy era.

BELOW:
Cotton Row today.

But the cotton market changed. Raw cotton is no longer necessary for samples; instead, a cotton classer sends a green card to a buyer. Many producers sell their cotton before it is even in the ground. Gradually the noise and cheerful chaos of Cotton Row began to disappear; the buildings began to decay, paint began to peel and windows crusted over with dirt.

Then came the renaissance of downtown Memphis. In 1978 the Cotton Row Historic District, which included the cobblestone river landing, was declared by the Memphis Landmarks Commission. The old warehouses have become restaurants, the sky-lit classing rooms have been converted into condominiums or studios. Cotton bales are still seen on the streets occasionally, but business is done in air-conditioned offices. The new denizens of Cotton Row are bringing a vigor to the area by remembering its heritage.

SAME OLD GAME

On Front Street lives the cotton buyer,
He's called a thief, he's called a liar,
He says if he should have to pay
The price you ask for cotton today
He might as well his business sell
And spend his days in darkest hell.

On Front Street lives the cotton seller,
In some respects a decent fellow,
He says the mills don't pay enough
To keep his customers in snuff,
He says the profits mills are making
From downtrodden farmers they are taking.

From other sections come the spinners
Who say they often skip their dinners
In order to economize
Which sounds to me like a lot of lies.

But statistics show the farmer planting
Still more cotton, tho' still he's ranting
About the awful cost of labor
And cussing out his next door neighbor
And accusing him of profits stopping
Because he pays so much for chopping,
And in the fall when things are clicking,
He cusses about the cost of picking.

The laborer says he cannot live
On what the farmers want to give
As daily wages for the toil
Of this poor tiller of the soil.

But every year the crop is made,
And every year the game is played
And most all of them are satisfied
Tho' bound to admit that they have lied,
And their satisfaction only lacks
The getting by on income tax.

April, 1948

From *FRONT STREET*
* A Book of Poems by William Johnstone Britton

GAYOSO-PEABODY

The Gayoso-Peabody District, a five block area east of Front Street including Main and Second Streets between McCall and Monroe, grew in proximity to and because of Cotton Row. Hotels, saloons, restaurants, grocers, hardware and dry goods merchants, and muletraders all located in the area between Cotton Row and the central business district several blocks north to serve the needs of the people from all over the South who came to buy and sell cotton.

The area takes its name from two famous hotels: the Gayoso (1842) and the Peabody (1869) which once stood as the focal points of the district. Though both buildings are gone now, there are many remnants of Gay Nineties ebullience. The remaining buildings, dating from 1880 to the 1920s, are characterized by diversity and eclecticism; a variety of architectural styles — Richardsonian Romanesque, Italianate Victorian, even Art Deco — may be seen. But the uniform setback from the street and the similarity in height (mostly five and six stories), as well as the use of cast iron and terra cotta decorations, give a cohesiveness to the area. In contrast to the utilitarian simplicity of the Cotton Row buildings, the gaiety and decoration of the Gayoso-Peabody buildings were designed to lure shoppers and travellers.

 Today the first floors have been remodelled with blue glass, chrome and plastic, but by looking up to the top floors one can see reminders of the nineteenth century. ∎

DOWNTOWN CHURCHES

In the first half of the nineteenth century Memphis provided the only port city between St. Louis and New Orleans and was earning a reputation as a rough and ready harbor for river boatmen. Their commerce was vital to the new city's existence, and churches were not among their top priorities. But as more settlers arrived, religion and respectability grew, and the second half of the century saw the building of several handsome churches representing various denominations.

Two architects played important roles in building the houses of worship: James B. Cook and Edward C. Jones.

James B. Cook (1828-1909) was a British immigrant who had worked as supervising architect of the Crystal Palace before coming to New York in 1855. He had studied architecture and civil engineering at King's College and Putney College in England. Two years after his arrival in New York he moved to Memphis, bringing "modern" knowledge and skill to the frontier. He served in the Confederate Army. He was responsible for the 1881 renovation of Calvary Episcopal, the design and completion of Trinity Lutheran, and the building of St. Mary's Catholic churches. He was also responsible for the Pyramid which represented Memphis in the Tennessee Centennial Exposition in Nashville in 1896, and was the designer of submarines and patented jail systems.

Edward Culliatt Jones (1822-1902) was the architect of First Presbyterian, Second Presbyterian (now Clayborn Temple), and Beale Street Baptist churches, as well as many other homes and commercial buildings. Born in Charleston, South Carolina, and educated there and in Northampton, Massachusetts, he began his career in Charleston in 1848, designing several buildings of note there. He, too, served in the Confederate Army, and in 1866 decided to move west to Memphis. His first work in Memphis was remodeling seven stores at Main and Monroe, known as the Brinkley Block. He was soon busy designing commercial buildings, churches, elaborate mansions and more modest dwellings. In an 1883 *Review* of local biographies, he was described as being "considered a most important member of the community, not only as a meritorious scientific artist, but also as a citizen, having the respect, esteem and confidence of the community."

Jones' career spanned many types and styles of buildings, from simple dwellings to the first skyscraper south of the Ohio River, the D. T. Porter building on Court Square. James A. Patrick, author of *Architecture in Tennessee*, said in a 1980 interview:

> What is extraordinary is that the career of the architect, E.C. Jones, spanned two very different ages. He had first designed buildings in Charleston in the Greek Revival style. That means that he would have originally been working with tools and techniques used in the 16th Century, and some which can be traced back to the Roman Empire. It's a testimony to the versatility of architects like Jones that he made the transition from these venerable techniques to steel and rivets. It is also an indication of how quickly fundamental changes took place in this country. ∎

Calvary Episcopal Church   1843

The congregation of Calvary Episcopal Church, the oldest public building in Memphis, traces its beginnings to services held on a flatboat in 1832 by the Reverend Thomas Wright. The arrival of the Reverend Philip Alston from North Carolina in 1839 meant that the congregation grew and was soon crowded in its simple frame chapel. By 1842 an article in the *American Eagle* stated that the Episcopal Church was contemplating a new building but waiting for money to accumulate before beginning. The money must have come in quickly, because in 1843 construction began on a church measuring one hundred feet by forty-eight feet, capable of seating six hundred people. Philip Alston drew the plans himself, and builder W. A. Bickford executed them on a lot at the corner of Second and Adams.

The original floor plan was symmetrical, with brick walls, a flat ceiling and no chancel. The tower was added in 1848. Alston was no architect, as is shown by the fact that the roof gave way within four years, but he had a fine sense of proportion. His boxlike building with pointed Gothic windows and steeply pitched roof represented a grand vision: to plan to seat six hundred worshippers in a town of barely two thousand people was showing faith in the Lord and in the future.

In 1881 extensive renovation was carried out by English-trained architect James B. Cook, which brought the interior design into keeping with Anglican ideas of worship. A chancel was added and the flat ceiling was opened to expose dark oak beams and the steep pitch of the roof. Alston had probably designed the ceiling flat because, to the taste of the early nineteenth century, the exposed beams would have looked like a reminder of frontier log cabins. Over the years the interior has changed little since the "modernization" of the 1880s, but twelve stained glass windows have been added as memorials.

The simplicity of the tall dark oak roof and white walls with simple arches of stained glass give the church a quiet dignity. In 1961 a stucco veneer, which had probably been applied prior to Cook's remodeling to give the appearance of stone, was removed, exposing the hand-made clay bricks.

Pew rentals provided financial support for the church from 1846 to 1907, and one of the silver nameplates is still in place. Today the congregation has established a trust fund to preserve and maintain the building.

Shields McIlwaine in *Memphis Down in Dixie* tells that Yankee General Sherman and his staff attended a service at Calvary shortly after the occupation of Memphis by Union forces in 1862. The minister intoned the ritual, but omitted the passage asking divine protection for the President of the United States. Thereupon, General Sherman leaped to his feet and loudly supplied the missing prayer. ∎

OPPOSITE RIGHT:
*The Gothic-style nave of
St. Peter's.*

BELOW:
*St. Peter's Roman
Catholic Church at 190
Adams, built in 1854.*

St. Peter's Roman Catholic Church

1854

A block away from Calvary at 190 Adams stands the second oldest church building in Memphis, St. Peter's Roman Catholic Church. The congregation was founded in 1840 and its first Dominican pastor was appointed in 1847. Father Michael McAleer had purchased the lot at Third and Adams for five hundred dollars in 1840, and a crude brick building was erected two years later. The present structure was begun in 1852 and built *around* the original building, which was dismantled and carried out the front doors when the new structure was completed in 1855. Two bishops dedicated the new church in 1858 before a congregation of two thousand worshippers.

The architect for St. Peter's was Patrick C. Keeley (1816-96) who designed over seven hundred Catholic churches. The fact that the designer was a professional architect shows in the building's considerable advancement over the simplicity of Calvary. The floor plan is cruciform, with arches, piers and vaulting. The church is not truly Gothic in that the vaulting has no structural value, but it uses Gothic motifs in its decoration.

It is a brick structure with stucco walls modeled to resemble stone. The exterior looks like a medieval fortress with a large center entry under a Gothic arched window and two octagonal towers with smaller entrances on either side of the facade. Arches are repeated in the towers, which are topped with battlements.

The richly colored interior has a nave with side aisles divided by clustered piers topped with gilded acanthus leaves. The windows are Bavarian stained glass.

When, in 1934, St. Peter's became the first church in Memphis to be air-conditioned, three iron caskets were discovered under the main altar. They contained the bodies of three priests, one who died of cholera and two of yellow fever after serving the city through its epidemics. They are memorialized in the entry. ∎

AT RIGHT:
*St. Mary's Roman
Catholic Church at
Market and Third, built
during the Civil War.*

St. Mary's
Roman Catholic Church

1 8 6 4

St. Mary's Roman Catholic Church was organized by the Franciscans in 1862 for German Catholics who had been worshipping at Irish-oriented St. Peter's. The cornerstone for the new church was laid in 1864 during Union occupation, and the Union military authorities cooperated in the ceremony, even firing off a cannon for the dedication. The architect was James B. Cook; thus, this is the first work by a local architect.

The church was dedicated in 1870, but work continued on the sanctuary until 1874, and the steeple remained incomplete until 1901. At some time a stucco coating was added, but, like Calvary, this was removed in 1971 to show the beauty of the original brick. The steeple was removed from the tower for structural reasons.

The facade has a central tower over the Third Street entrance. The windows, arches in the tower and even the pew ends repeat the pointed Gothic motif.

The interior is lighter and more graceful than that at St. Peter's and more brightly painted. The clustered piers are delicate, and over the entrance opposite the altar is a graceful choir loft which projects into the sanctuary like the bow of a ship. A delicate unsupported stair curves up to the choir. At the opposite end of the nave is the altar in a semi-circular apse.

The Grotto of Our Lady of Lourdes on the south side of the nave was completed in 1875, the gift of Kate Magevney Hamilton, daughter of Eugene Magevney, in whose house the first Catholic rites in Memphis were held. ∎

Trinity Lutheran Church

1874-88

Like St. Mary's, Trinity Lutheran Church was organized for German immigrants. Many Germans were coming to the United States, discouraged by developments in Germany: required military training, increasingly centralized government and restricted religious freedoms. By the 1850s German-speaking people were figuring prominently in the civic and social life of Memphis. In June of 1855 Pastor John R. Beyer arrived by steamboat from St. Louis and held a communion service for seventy-four people. The first services were held in the First Presbyterian Church at Third and Poplar; later the group worshipped in an upstairs room at City Hall, then located on Main between Market and Winchester for almost two decades.

In 1871 the group purchased a lot for $7,000 on Washington Avenue, then little more than a cowpath with hitching posts and cobblestones. The first story of a two-story plan was opened in 1874 and housed a parochial school as well as the church; but the upper story was not completed till 1878, and remained unfinished till 1888.

The yellow fever plagues of the 1870s greatly reduced the congregation's numbers. Ninety-nine members were listed in the church records as dying. Many Germans resettled in St. Louis, and the membership dwindled from six hundred to one hundred and forty. But work on the church continued. Services were conducted in German for many years.

James B. Cook was the architect, and his building has a Gothic flavor, designed in dark red brick with white limestone trim, a central tower ending in a small spire and pointed arch windows. In 1950 a permastone veneer was added, greatly changing the church's exterior appearance.

The sanctuary on the second floor retains much of its original look. Pointed window arches cross the nave to support the low pitched roof. Between the arches are Belz stained glass windows from Germany, memorials to members whose names reflect the German heritage: Baumann, Burwinkel, Borckmann, Uhlmann and Toensmann. The handsome hand-carved altar, standing in a semi-circular apse, was shipped from Dresden, Germany, in many pieces and assembled here. ■

ABOVE:
The carved altar from Germany at Trinity Lutheran Church, 210 Washington.

AT RIGHT:
The First Methodist Church silver communion service that was buried on the property during the Civil War.

First Methodist Church

1 8 8 7 - 9 3

Sharing the block with the First Presbyterian Church, but turning its face toward Second Street, is the First Methodist Church. The first preaching recorded in Memphis was done by a slave, Uncle Harry Lawrence, who preached to both blacks and whites at the corner of Main and Winchester around 1822. The first representative of an organized denomination arrived in 1826: the Reverend Thomas Davidson, a Methodist circuit rider, who organized the Methodist society and rode into Memphis to hold services every sixth Sunday.

Outdoor revival meetings, known as "brush arbor" meetings for the circle of branches erected to shelter the preacher, were an important part of frontier life, but they occured irregularly. In 1831 a fulltime minister, the Reverend Francis Owen, was sent to Memphis to shepherd a congregation of eleven members. By the next year the Methodists had built, at a cost of one hundred and fifty dollars, a log meeting house at Second and Poplar with two doors for men and women to enter separately. The Methodists were generous; their little frame building also sheltered services for the Baptists, the Episcopalians and the Presbyterians in their early days.

By 1843 the Methodists had outgrown the building. It was moved to the back of the lot and a new building begun. The period of the Civil War was a tumultuous one for the congregation. The minister enlisted in the Confederate Army and the United States government asssigned a preacher to take his place. Most of the congregation refused to attend his services, so the

Presbyterians shared their meeting facilities next door. A silver communion service owned by the church since 1855 was buried on the property to keep it safe from the Yankee soldiers.

In May, 1887, ground was broken for a new church on the same location. The plans were purchased from an architect named Jacob Snyder of Akron, Ohio. Called the "Akron plan," it featured Sunday school rooms at the rear of the auditorium. The foundation walls are Alabama limestone and Arkansas ironstone. Above the floor line the walls are rough gray granite, with a roof and spire of slate. This departure from the usual brick was made possible by improved means of transportation, railways and steamships, which enabled the heavy building materials to be moved long distances.

A Bible, photographs, current papers and a bottle of River Jordan water were placed in the cornerstone. The ceremony marking this was not without excitement; the derrick holding up the heavy stone got its ropes tangled on the roof of a passing street car and the audience scattered in all directions before order was restored. The church was completed in 1893.

The facade faces west on Second and has double doors under a central arch of lighter stone. Horizontal bands of the lighter stone divide the facade. Like its neighbor the Presbyterian Church, the building has a recessed tower to the right of the entrance; the tower holds a clock made in Troy, New York.

While the exterior is virtually unchanged from the original drawings, the interior has been remodelled several times to suit changing needs. ∎

AT LEFT:
*First Methodist Church
at 204 North Second,
built in 1887.*

First Presbyterian Church   1 8 8 4

 A missionary to the Chickasaw Indians and five devoted followers organized the first Presbyterian church in Memphis in 1828. For a while they shared a crude meeting house with the Methodists and Baptists, and in 1832 the Mayor and Aldermen deeded an old cemetery lot at the corner of Poplar and Third to the Presbyterians. A brick building was completed two years later and by 1845 there were two hundred and forty-eight white and forty-six black members. The growth of the congregation required an even bigger building in 1854.

In 1862 General Grant's army seized the building and nailed the Stars and Stripes over the door, preventing the congregation from meeting for a time. The minister of the time, refusing to pass under the Union flag, put a ladder up to a back window and entered the church that way. In 1873, the first of that decade's four yellow fever epidemics struck, killing many members of the church. The minister contracted yellow fever ministering to the sick and died in 1873. At the very hour of his funeral, the roof of the church collapsed. Lives were spared because the funeral was being held at the cemetery to prevent further infection. Still another trial was in the offing for the church — a disastrous fire destroyed the whole structure in 1883.

The congregation triumphed over these disasters, and in 1884, less than a year after the fire, a new building had been erected on the same spot, the one we see today. E. C. Jones designed this third church building in a Norman style, reflecting the less ornate, more conservative church architecture of the late nineteenth century.

The facade, facing Poplar on the south, is brick, stone and terra cotta, divided into three sections by buttresses. The center entrance is emphasized with double doors set in a round arch with a fan transom. The arches and windows have vari-colored brick and terra cotta decoration. The clay springers and keystones have molded sunflowers on them. On the east, recessed from the front, is a square tower which once had a steeple. After the steeple was removed, the base was refashioned into a Romanesque style belfry.

The sanctuary is on the second floor above the Sunday School rooms. Its arrangement is like that of a New England style meeting house with the pulpit on a rostrum at the center front of the room. Since the church was built, many changes in interior decoration have occured, but Jones' ceiling design — an unusual arrangement of large geometric patterns formed by heavy wooden moldings — remains.

The most striking feature of the interior is the tall vestibule. One enters a low ceilinged dark area and is immediately drawn to a wide, well-lighted stairway on the left. The wainscoting of the stairway and the dark high-pitched ceiling and the stained glass window giving light on the second level, give an impression of great height and draw one up to the entry to the sanctuary. ∎

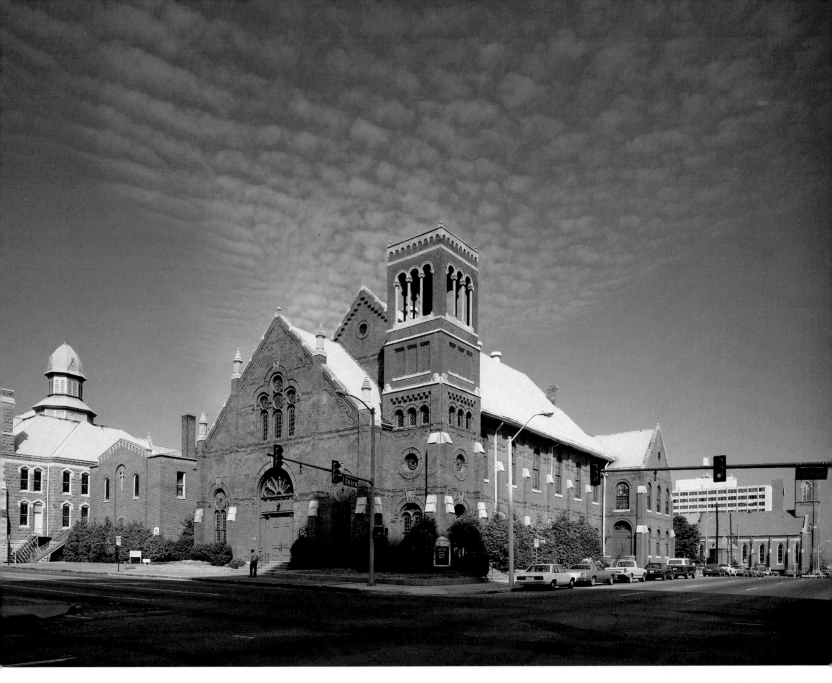

ABOVE:
First Presbyterian Church (1884) at the corner of Poplar and Third with First Methodist on the left and St. Mary's on the right.

AT RIGHT:
*Clayborn Temple at
Hernando and Pontotoc,
built in 1891 as Second
Presbyterian Church.*

1891

Clayborn Temple

(formerly Second Presbyterian Church)

The Second Presbyterian Church, now Clayborn Temple, is contemporary with First Methodist, and like that church and Beale Street Baptist, involved E. C. Jones in its building. Church records show that the plans were drawn by the firm of Kees and Long of Minneapolis, but E. C. Jones of Memphis was supervising architect. The lot at Pontotoc and Hernando was purchased by the congregation in 1888 for $14,000 and the church was dedicated in 1891. In 1949 the building was sold to the African Methodist Episcopal Church and renamed Clayborn Temple, for John Henry Clayborn, Bishop of the A.M.E. Church.

This building was the site of many civil rights rallies in the 1960s and many of the marches of the sanitation workers' strike began here.

The exterior has changed little although a spire on the tower was removed in 1924. It is cream stone with arched windows and entrances leading one visually to the tower, which has three windows on each side near the top and small pinnacles around the cornice.

The floor plan is unique in nineteenth century Memphis churches. The auditorium, which seats two thousand, runs diagonally to the square floor plan. The pulpit, in a half-dome niche, is in the opposite corner from the tower and pews radiate from the rostrum. There are entrances in the other three corners and a balcony circling the walls, giving the room a fan-shaped arrangement. ∎

BEALE STREET

"If Beale Street could talk . . ." wrote W. C. Handy in the song that was to carry the street's fame around the world. The street that stretches for a mile and a third east from the Mississippi River has a colorful tale to tell.

In 1838 Robertson Topp and his partners purchased land south of the town of Memphis' southern boundary at Union Avenue and laid out streets, including Beale. Their investment was meant as a rival to Memphis and called South Memphis by its proprietors, "Sodom" by its detractors. At first South Memphis was mainly residential. George Wyatt built a Greek Revival mansion, and Topp and others built handsome homes along Beale. The proprietors tried to lure businesses into their town, and Topp opened the grand Gayoso Hotel in 1843. In 1846 South Memphis was incorporated as a town, and its mayor, J.T. Trezevant, led a campaign for consolidation. After a referendum, Memphis and South Memphis were united in 1859 with a population of 8,841.

The steamboat landing at the foot of Beale made it a busy place, and hotels for merchants and travellers as well as saloons for the roustabouts and crews grew up. In 1853 the Memphis and Charleston Railroad used a depot at the east end of Beale as its terminus, insuring the street's importance. In 1859 the city opened South Market House, built at a cost of $5,000, on the site of what is now Handy Park. As early as 1851 a black owned property on Beale; in October a free Negro named Joe Clouston bought a lot at Beale and DeSoto (now Fourth). With the wharf, warehouses, stores, hotels, saloons, and elegant residences, Beale Street was a bustling thoroughfare.

During the Union occupation of Memphis during the Civil War, Beale Street saw another kind of activity. General Grant established his headquarters at the Hunt (once the Wyatt) home on Beale, ensuring the traffic of Federal soldiers, while the landing on the river saw the passage of much contraband.

After the war, a Freedman's school operated for a time in the Hunt home, and fraternal orders sprang up for the aid of the newly freed Negroes. Beale Street for many years was the first stopping place for blacks going north. The street witnessed tragedy: the activities of the Ku Klux Klan and, by one account, the incident which started the race riot of 1866 occurred at Beale and Main.

But the post-war years brought peaceful changes, too. By the 1870s Beale Street had a sizable black population, and the cornerstone of Beale Street Baptist Church was laid in 1871. One of the most important newcomers was Robert Church. He had been a steward on a riverboat at the outbreak of the war, and put that experience to good use by getting a job in a saloon on Beale. Soon he was able to open his own saloon, and he used the profits to buy property, becoming Memphis' first black millionaire by the time of his death in 1912.

When Memphis faced insolvency in 1879, a black man was one of the first to step forward to aid the city's recovery. Robert Church purchased, for $1,000, the first bond issued in 1881. Church was the leader of the black community on Beale, and he provided the Negroes with their first park. He built a park, playground and community center with trees, shady walks, benches and picnic tables on land near the Beale Street Baptist Church, and, in 1899, opened Church's Auditorium which quickly became a focal point for the black community. It seated two thousand people, and Booker T. Washington, W. E. B. Du Bois and Theodore Roosevelt spoke there.

The legend of Beale Street grew between 1880 and the First World War. The street was a patchwork: near the river were warehouses and businesses related to shipping; from the Opera House at Main to Third Street were white business; from Third to Turley was the Negro business section; further east were the mansions of white businessmen, while at the eastern end of the street were black residences. It is the three block area that was called "the Main Street of Negro America" that created the legend.

Here businesses owned by or catering to Negroes grew: undertaking parlors, stores, restaurants and insurance companies. From them a small but select Negro middle class developed, many of whom lived on South Lauderdale near Beale. But the street was cosmopolitan; Jews had owned clothing and department stores there since the 1850s, Italians set up saloons and theaters, and a Chinese Masonic Lodge was established above a laundry on Beale in 1890.

But it was the entertainment and the less-than-legitimate activities that gave Beale its fame. Beale Street at night became a refuge from the oppression of prejudice and segregation. In *Beale Black and Blue*, McKee and Chisenhall say, "The white man had said that the black man couldn't go certain places, that Beale was the place for blacks; and the black man turned it around and said Beale was the *only* place to be."

There were saloons and bars and gambling dens alongside the stores and funeral parlors. A former resident remembers eight or ten pawnshops in the three block area. Gamblers and pimps and prostitutes rubbed shoulders with young men fresh from the country, wide-eyed at the flashy dress of the city slickers. After the hard work of the day, people were ready to enjoy themselves in the cool of the evening, and the street never closed down.

There were always crowds you had to elbow your way through. Street vendors sold live chickens, buckets of sticky sorghum and ripe blackberries in season. Photographers would take your tintype, a fortune teller would tell your future, herb doctors would sell potions to cure any ill or cast any spell. There were the smells: barbecue, fish frying and chitlins.

And the music. Always the music: bands in the theaters or on street corners, a lone musician practicing in a rented room over a store, translating the blues of the Delta farmhand into a language that would move the world. It was this atmosphere into which W. C. Handy came soon after the turn of the century, and from which his music would spread far beyond Beale Street.

AT LEFT:
*Schwab's Dry Goods
Store on Beale has been
operated by the same
family since 1876, one of
the few unchanging
landmarks on the street.*

First Baptist Beale Street

1 8 7 1

The famous statue that impressed W. C. Handy is no longer on the tower of First Baptist Church Beale Street, and time has brought many other changes, but the structure is still an impressive one. The oldest black congregation in Memphis traces its history back to 1854, to "praise meetings" held in the home of the Reverend Scott Keys on Beale near Turley. The worshippers met in a number of other buildings, including the basement of a white church at Main and Beale, until 1863, when the American Baptist Home Mission Society of New York donated the property on Beale. A stone building was erected there, but burned in 1865.

In 1871 the cornerstone for the present building, designed by Edward C. Jones and M.H. Baldwin, was laid. Tradition says that the building cost $100,000 and was paid for immediately. Tradition exaggerates. The truth is nearer $12,000, which still made it one of the most expensive churches of the time, and work went on for twenty-two years as the congregation raised the money. The weekly *Free Speech* was published at First Baptist Beale in the 1890s, with Ida B. Wells' fiery anti-lynching editorials.

Financial worries continued to plague the church. In 1923 it was lost to creditors, and two congregations merged, changing the name to New Prospect Baptist Church. In 1925 a fire damaged the building, and when the property was repaired the members took back the original name of First Baptist Beale Street. Presidents Ulysses S. Grant and Theodore Roosevelt are said to have spoken at the church.

The auditorium occupies the entire second floor. Round arches support the roof and ample windows give light. An immersion baptistry is at the front and a gallery is on both sides and the back. The church has retained its original soft pastel colored glass windows.

Today the exterior has a Romanesque flavor, with three round-arched entrances beneath a multiple circular stained glass window and towers at each side of the facade. Much of the Victorian ornament has fallen off, giving it its present simplicity. The original plan included a pediment mounted by a tall cornice with scrolls and geometric patterns building to a crest topped by a cross. One tower had a cupola-like structure with square piers supporting arches topped by a Celtic cross. This structure fell into the nave, causing great damage, before 1885.

The galvanized tin statue of St. John the Baptist with his arm pointing heavenward topped the other tower. The statue was struck by lightning many times and lost one of its arms when a man, either angered by a split in the church or merely drunk, scaled the tower and cut off the arm. In 1938 the statue was dropped by workmen repairing lightning damage and too badly crumpled to be repaired. Thus Memphis lost one of its most notable landmarks.

If I were an artist I would long ago have given the world a painting, expressive of my emotion when a small boy on a visit to Memphis, I first saw Beale Street Baptist Church, with the hand of St. John the Baptist pointing heavenward enveloped in the snowflakes from the gray sky.

W. C. Handy, quoted in
George W. Lee's
*Beale Street,
Where the Blues Began.*

Hunt-Phelan House

1830-51

Wrapped in its cloak of trees like an aging beauty hiding from prying eyes stands one of Memphis' most interesting houses. The Hunt-Phelan House on Beale Street is distinguished both architecturally and because of its adventures in the Civil War.

The original part of the house was built about 1830 for George Hubbard Wyatt, a land office surveyor. It was a brick Federal style two-story house, each story consisting of four rooms and a central hall. There were stone lintels over each window and a small portico on the front, or north side, and a low-pitched roof. Wyatt's cousin, Jesse Minor Tate, also lived there.

In 1835 Colonel Eli Moore Driver, a retired land commissioner, bought the house, leaving it upon his death to his daughter Sarah Elizabeth and her husband, Colonel William Richardson Hunt. It has been in the possession of this family and their descendants, the Phelans, ever since.

In 1851 a two-story kitchen and service wing, containing servants' quarters, repair shops, wood storage, and laundry rooms was added at the back, connected to the main house by a two-story porch. The small portico was moved to the east side entrance and a more imposing portico in Greek Revival Style was added on the north. The wooden cornice and architrave are supported by four fluted Ionic columns with cast iron caps which were shipped by river from Cairo, Illinois.

The property originally covered an entire block, with the house in the center, surrounded by barns, stables, smokehouses, brick cottages for slaves and a schoolhouse for them. On the west side was a small building housing a furnace which burned resin and cottonseed to produce illumination gas for the main house. About twenty-four hours of steady burning were required to generate enough gas to light the house for one evening's entertainment.

The grounds and gardens were laid out by a French architect, with lily pools, green house, vegetable gardens, and small fruit trees. The lawn had walks, driveways, shrubbery and fine trees. Surrounding the grounds was a hedge of Cherokee roses.

One story from the house's early days tells of the time that young Miss Julia Driver was practicing her piano scales in the parlor. In the sourrounding woods an Indian heard the strange sounds and wandered into the house to see what caused them. Miss Julia, though frightened, kept playing, and was much relieved when he gave a satisfied nod and left.

Colonel Driver had to ride his horse "Gold Mine" along a muddy, rough lane (later known as Beale Street) to get to town. He died in 1851 and is buried in Elmwood Cemetery.

His son-in-law, Colonel William R. Hunt, owned the house during the Civil War. He volunteered for combat duty but President Jefferson Davis wrote him that his technical services were "worth more than 50,000 men to the Southern Cause," and assigned him to the large Atlanta arsenal, after which he commanded the arsenal at Montgomery, Alabama.

The "Fighting Bishop" of the Confederacy, General Leonidas Polk, was a friend of the family and stayed in the house in the first months of the war. From the library he organized the Provisional Army of Tennessee and planned his battles.

Barely escaping from LaGrange, Tennessee, before General Nathan Bedford Forrest came, General Ulysses S. Grant seized the house for Union headquarters in late June, 1862, after the fall of Memphis. Grant used the house as his headquarters after the Battle of Shiloh in July of that year, and planned the Vicksburg campaign in the library. When Mrs. Grant visited, she stayed in the house, but General Grant slept in a tent pitched under a tree in the front yard.

Mrs. Hunt had been allowed to take one carload of furniture and possessions from the house when the Yankees seized it. She followed her husband around the Confederacy with her boxcar of possessions. When the Hunts returned after the war, they found that the house was bare, and their much-travelled carload of belongings (some of which remain in the house today) was all they had. During his tenancy, General Grant had seen to it that the laws of war were observed in his headquarters and kept his officers from taking things, but he was attracted to Hunt's fine barometer and kept it in his tent throughout the war. After Grant moved on, other officers were not so careful.

Mrs. Elizabeth Meriwether tells in her *Recollections of Ninety-two Years* about going to Grant's headquarters at the Hunt home. Her husband was away serving in the Confederate Army, and a neighbor, fearing for the safety of Mrs. Meriwether and her children, had offered her the protection of his gardener and his wife, who moved into the detached kitchen at the Meriwether home. The gardener's wife, a brawny Irishwoman named Mrs. Hickey, soon set up a saloon in Mrs. Meriwether's kitchen to serve the Union soldiers. Nothing Mrs. Meriwether could say or do would budge Mrs. Hickey, who claimed the property as her own on the grounds that Mr. Meriwether was a Confederate officer while she and her husband were loyal Union sympathizers. When Mrs. Meriwether protested, Mrs. Hickey threatened her with a carving knife.

Mrs. Meriwether took her case to General Grant and was escorted into the Hunt library, where the general was seated at a table with an unlit cigar in his mouth. He listened to her story, then wrote a note, saying, "Give this to the Provost Marshall." Mrs. Hickey was evicted, and Mrs. Meriwether was safe in her home. But not for long, for hers was one of the first families ordered out of town by General Sherman's eviction orders of 1862.

After Grant's departure, General T. C. Hamilton occupied the house, and had it bristling with big guns. A powder magazine was located in the tunnel cellar of the house and there were trench tunnels from each entrance to the roads, as well as a camouflaged mortar at the gate. The fortifications were meant as protection against Forrest's Raiders. One raid occurred in early September, 1864, when some Confederates galloped by and fired a salvo at Yankee officers on the porch. Some said the Yankees ran all the way to Fort Pickering.

ABOVE:
The Hunt-Phelan house was built in the 1830s and the portico added in 1851.

From February of 1863 to August of 1865, the house was used as a hospital operated by the Western Sanitary Commission under Mr. O. E. Waters. The victims of Sherman's bloody battles were cared for in the ell at the rear of the home. Thousands of disabled Union soldiers stayed there and barracks were erected on the grounds.

Upon hearing stories about starving drummer boys, some ladies from St. Louis came and organized relief for privates on furlough. Their efforts were part of the Association for Relief of Misery on the Battlefields, a predecessor of the American Red Cross.

The Hunts and their carload of possesions returned at the end of the war, but later left again, this time driven out by the yellow fever epidemic of 1873. They and their daughter's family fled to Louisville, Kentucky, where William Richardson Hunt Phelan was christened in the arms of Mrs. Jefferson Davis with Mr. Davis standing close by. The Davises were living in Memphis after the war, and like their friends the Hunts and the Phelans, had fled from the yellow fever.

Again in 1878 the family left to escape the fever. They left the house under the protection of Uncle Nathan Wilson, a former slave and faithful servant who had buried the family silver to protect it from the Union troops.

Elder Blair T. Hunt, a distinguished black educator in Memphis, recalled before his death that his father and grandfather had lived in the servants quarters on the Hunt place. ∎

AT RIGHT:
The Hunt-Phelan house as it was used as a hospital for Federal troops in 1863.

SOLDIERS HOME MEMPHIS TENN.
ESTABLISHED BY THE WESTERN SANITARY COMMISSION FEBRUARY 1st 1863

ADAMS AVENUE

The best place to look at the architecture of Memphis' past is Adams Avenue. The western end of Adams was the public landing stage in the nineteenth century, so the street became a busy thoroughfare. Two early churches, Calvary Episcopal and St. Peter's Catholic, still border Adams, and are now surrounded by skyscrapers and government buildings. The Magevney House, one of the oldest residences still standing, with its white paint and green shutters, brings a taste of almost rural simplicity. A little further east stands a collection of Victorian townhouses, three now lending their dignity to law offices, with one still a home. Still further east, the tall magnolias and the turreted mansions of Victorian Village recall the exuberence of the Gay Nineties.

Magevney House

1 8 3 0 s

One of the oldest homes in Memphis is the simple frame cottage belonging to Eugene Magevney at 198 Adams. It is open to the public as a museum and provides a glimpse of family life in the early days of the city.

Eugene Magevney was a young Catholic immigrant from County Fermagh, Ireland, who arrived in Memphis in 1834 and began to teach school in a log cabin in Court Square. He boarded with a man named William McKeon and saved his money, in 1837 buying the clapboard cottage on Adams from John Manning. The house on the seventy-five foot by one hundred and forty-eight foot lot must have been recently built when Magevney bought the property because Manning had paid only two hundred and fifty dollars for it in 1835 and two years later sold it to Magevney for two thousand five hundred dollars.

The house was originally a four-room structure, with two rooms and a hall downstairs and two rooms upstairs which were accessible only from the outside. A second bedroom and dining room were added in a wing at the back during the 1850s. The roof is cypress shingles and the exterior is painted white with green shutters. Part of the pine flooring is original, as are the doors, brass nameplate and key to the front door. There were three outbuildings on the property: a carriage house, separate kitchen and servants' quarters. Part of the original brick wall surrounds the back of the lot.

By 1840 Magevney had saved enough money to send to Ireland for his fiancee, Mary Smyth, who had been waiting for him for twelve years. The trunk that she brought with her from Ireland is still in the house. When their marriage was celebrated in the house in 1840, it was the first Catholic wedding in Memphis, and it was followed by the first Catholic baptism in 1841.

Magevney taught school for only six years but he prospered through real estate investments, and became a city alderman, in which capacity he was instrumental in organizing the city school system in 1848. He was a pillar of the Catholic community and helped found St. Peter's Catholic Church. The first mass in Memphis was said in his home. The dresser which served as the altar for these early masses is on display at the house; it is a heavy walnut-finished American Empire piece with claw feet and hand-blown glass drawer pulls.

The Magevneys had two daughters, Mary, born in 1841, and Kate, born in 1842. Mary joined the Dominican Order of Nuns and started the Sacred Heart Convent in Galveston, Texas. Kate was married twice, to John Dawson in 1867, and after his death, to Hugh Hamilton in 1882. She lived with both her husbands in the house on Adams. Kate had one adopted daughter, Blanche Hamilton, an orphan who had been raised by the nuns at Sacred Heart. When Mary Magevney died in 1891, Blanche was sent to Memphis and adopted by Kate in 1897.

Eugene Magevney died of yellow fever in 1873 and his wife survived him till 1889. When her father died, Kate took over the management of his investments, and by the time she died in 1930, the estate was worth over three and a half million dollars. She gave generously to local Catholic charities and her gifts helped start St. Joseph Hospital, the Grotto of Lourdes at St. Mary's Catholic Church, and the infant wing at St. Peter's Orphanage; she gave land at the corner of Poplar and Cleveland to Christian Brothers College.

AT LEFT:
The Magevney House at 198 Adams, built in the 1830s, is open to the public.

When Kate died, she left no will, and there was a prolonged legal battle over the estate. The descendants of Eugene Magevney's brothers and sisters who had joined him in this country felt they were entitled to the money, and questioned whether Blanche's adoption was legal. The Convent, now moved to Houston, felt that it deserved some of the money through its founder, Mary Magevney. Eventually the dispute was settled, with some of the money going to the Convent. Mrs. Blanche Hamilton Karsh inherited the house on Adams, and in 1940 she donated it to the city. It has been restored and was opened as a museum in 1941. Many of the possessions of the Magevneys have been returned to the house, including a what-not, a canopy bed, a secretary, a papier-mache table, Magevney's school desk, altar cloths hand worked by Kate Magevney, and family portraits.

The simple frame house represents a long span of Memphis history since it was continuously lived in for one hundred years. From the early days when the Magevney family, two boarders, and five slaves crowded the property to its ownership by the eccentric Mrs. Hamilton, who always dressed in black and was known as a miser despite her great wealth, the house on Adams has seen Memphis through frontier days, Civil War, yellow fever plagues, booms and depressions, to modern times.

■

AT RIGHT:
The stairway in the First James Lee House, 1868.

First James Lee House

1868-69

James Lee, Jr., was the son of Captain James Lee, owner of the famous Lee Line of riverboats. James Lee, Jr., was born in Dover, Tennessee, and educated at the University of Nashville and Princeton. He moved to Memphis in 1858 to practice maritime law in a firm called Vollentine and Lee. He also served as vice-president of the Memphis Board of Fire and Police Commissioners, was involved in the Memphis Merchants Exchange, a bank and many other civic and business enterprises. By 1877 the younger Lee had retired from his law practice to take over his father's riverboat business.

In 1868 the younger Lee purchased a fifty foot lot now numbered 239 Adams, and engaged Joseph Willis, a Philadelphia architect who had moved to Memphis in 1858, to build him a house. The 1870 City Directory shows the family living there. As James Lee, Sr., became more infirm he moved into the house with his son, and died there in 1889. For thirty days after Captain Jim's death all steamboats coming into Memphis lowered their flags to half-mast in tribute.

His son, James Jr., prospered in business and civic affairs, and in his family. By the time he and his wife had six children the house at 239 Adams was too small, and in 1890 he purchased the much larger house on the corner of Adams and Orleans, and there the family, increased to ten children, lived till 1925.

The First Lee House is interesting for its connection with the famous riverboat family, and for its architecture, remarkably unchanged since the house has been lived in by only two families before its present use as law offices. The Quackenbush family rented the house from Lee before buying it in 1919. Mrs. Lottie Quackenbush Gamble lived there till her death in 1977.

Willis designed the house in Italianate Victorian style, with a side hall plan. The base of the house is stone, with stone marking the second-story line. The bold cornice has paired console brackets marking each of three bays. The roof is hipped standing seam metal. The entrance is reached by a flight of limestone steps and has a bracket-supported pediment. The windows have ornamented pediments. There are three wrought iron ventilation grills under the cornice.

The vestibule is floored with encaustic tile. The door has an etched glass panel and transom; the panel is a picture of Ceres with sheaves of wheat. The carved panelling on the door was probably done by steamboat carpenters, and includes anchors, ropes and marine motifs.

On the west are two parlors on the first floor, separated by massive panelled sliding doors. A staircase curves around the east wall of the entrance hall and has an octagonal newel post, twisted posts and scroll carving on the risers. An unusual curved wall in the front room on both floors echoes the curve of the stairway.

Throughout the house are heavy moldings. Only one ceiling medallion, in the dining room, remains. The mantel facings are cast iron grained to simulate marble. The windows have heavy casings and interior shutters.

A modern architect said the house was built "with knowing hand and restraint for the usually ebullient ornament common at the time."

■

John S. Toof House

1876

AT LEFT:
*The John S. Toof house
on Adams, 1876,
designed by Mathias
Harvey Baldwin.*

Mathias Harvey Baldwin was the architect for the house at 246 Adams. Baldwin had come to Memphis at age twenty-six in 1858. His name is usually coupled with that of Edward Culliatt Jones, with whom he shared a partnership from 1869 to 1879, but the Toof House on Adams was the work of Baldwin alone.

John S. Toof had arrived in Memphis five years before Baldwin, when he was only seventeen. He came from Ohio, and immediately found work on *The Memphis Whig* newspaper. Only two years later he became editor of *The Memphis Morning Bulletin*. In 1859 he retired from "the pencil field" to organize the Chamber of Commerce and was elected its secretary and superintendent. In 1862, while Memphis was occupied by Union troops, he went into the wholesale grocery and cotton factoring business. In 1873 he was central to the organization of the Memphis Cotton Exchange, again serving as secretary and superintendent. His organizational talents also played a part in the beginnings of the Memphis Water Company, and after the yellow fever epidemic of 1873 he was one of a committee studying the city's drainage system.

One of his contributions was to collate and print in intelligent form the annual reports of trade and commerce, and to issue daily reports of prices, stocks and imports of cotton and other commodities. He died in 1916 at the age of eighty.

In 1873 Toof purchased a thirty-six foot lot on the north side of Adams Avenue for $2,600 and engaged Baldwin to design a residence. Baldwin designed a typical three-story urban house of brick and stucco. The facade features a projecting brick-arched portico topped by galvanized iron and sheet metal scrolls and finials. The cornices are supported by large ornamental brackets of metal. On the first floor are two single segmentally arched floor-length windows with ornamental hood molds. The second floor has three four-paned windows and the third floor has one similar window with ornamental hood and three single bull's-eye windows.

A projecting bay on the west side extends for all three stories. An open porch wraps around the north side. The interior features a side hall plan. The third floor consists of only one long north-south room. The iron mantelpieces and shallow coal-burning fireplaces are original, as are most of the patterned brass door locks. Staircase risers are decorated with rope trim. ■

1 8 5 0 s

Fowlkes-Boyle House

The handsome Italianate Victorian townhouse at 208 Adams was built in the 1850s by Sterling Fowlkes. It is painted brick with brick quoins emphasizing the corners and limestone belt courses indicating the first and second floors. The cornice is supported by large paired brackets and incorporates cast iron ventilation grills in its design. The long windows on the front facade have ornate hoods. The structure has two stories, an attic and a basement, and is presently used as law offices.

Sterling Fowlkes and other members of his family came to Memphis from Virginia before 1840. He became a cotton factor and merchant. In 1851 an advertisement boasted, "S. & J. Fowlkes, located at Main and Adams, report that their last shipment of fine millinery took only eight days to arrive here from New York via fast express."

One of his sons, Sterling, Junior, was educated in Virginia and was already head of his own firm of cotton brokers when the Civil War broke out. He served in the Confederate Army and was promoted to a captaincy before he was killed in the Battle of Perryville at the age of twenty-five.

His father died at the age of sixty-nine in 1872. The Elmwood Cemetery records said of Sterling Fowlkes and his cousin Austin Fowlkes that they were "alike distinguished for probity and sterling integrity. They bent neither in the presence of adversity nor of prosperity and were ever the same honest, truthful, industrious merchants."

After Fowlkes' death the house was sold to Thomas Raymond Boyle, who was born in 1818 in County Leithrim, Ireland. Boyle and his brother John came to the United States to join a brother in the western gold rush, but stopped in Whiteville, Tennessee, where Thomas married Mary Jane Love in 1841, but she soon died without heirs. In 1847, Thomas Boyle married Margaret Owen, the sixteen-year-old daughter of Benjamin Owen from Owensville, Kentucky. The Boyle brothers sold lots in Whiteville, and their sister Honora joined them, marrying a cousin of Margaret Owen. In 1870 Thomas sold a plantation that his wife had inherited from her father and moved his family to Memphis. He and his wife had six children. After Thomas Boyle died of typhoid fever in 1890, his wife and children lived on in the house on Adams until 1920.

AT RIGHT:
*The Mette house,
designed by M.H.
Baldwin and E.C. Jones
in 1872.*

Mette House

1872

Mathias Harvey Baldwin and his partner Edward Culliatt Jones designed the two-story brick townhouse at 253 Adams in 1872. The cornice is supported by four pairs of carved wood brackets on the facade and a pair on each side wall. The corners of the house give the effect of stone quoins by raised courses of brick. Tall front windows have segmentally arched heads topped by cast cement hollow caps. Simple square brick columns hold an entry door pediment. The brick is laid in "English Garden Wall" pattern, then new in Memphis, and the walls are fourteen inches thick.

The first floor consisted of a parlor and dining room, and a hall with a lovely spindled staircase with scrolled carvings on each stair riser. Originally each room had a fireplace; two original black iron mantels can be seen in the upstairs rooms, now the library for a law firm.

The house was built for Herman Henry Mette, a German who arrived in Memphis by 1849 after having lived in Illinois and Cincinnati. He was a grocer, a bank director, and a prominent Catholic. He was one of the donors of the land for St. Mary's School at Third and Market, and in 1870 he persuaded the Franciscan monks in Illinois to send two priests to Memphis to take charge of St. Mary's. One of his sons, Martin Herman Mette, went into the dry goods business with John Gerber on Main Street in 1892.

In 1855 Mette bought a twenty-five foot lot on Adams and built a house which is no longer standing. In 1872 he commissioned architects Jones and Baldwin to build a house next door, now numbered 253 Adams. Mette and his wife chose to stay in their original residence, where he died in 1874 of yellow fever. Although Mette never lived at 253 Adams, it remained in his family for eighty years. His daughter Christina, her husband George Herbers, also a wholesale grocer, and their six children lived there till 1896.

At the turn of the century, the house stood vacant, then began a series of tenants, and a time as a rooming house. In 1952 the last family member to hold title sold the house. In 1968 it was extensively renovated and a wing added at the back, making its conversion to law offices.

∎

. VICTORIAN VILLAGE .
HISTORIC DISTRICT

The breeze rustles the magnolia leaves. One can almost hear the clip clop of carriage horses and the swish of taffeta petticoats of ladies coming to pay late afternoon calls. The shaded block of Adams Avenue is a world . . . but only a few blocks . . . away from the skyscrapers of downtown Memphis. But to go there on a summer afternoon is to step back in time. It is Victorian Village, a living museum of Memphis' past.

Mallory-Neely House

1 8 5 2 - 9 0

The Gay Nineties live again for the visitor to the Mallory-Neely House at 652 Adams. It is easy to imagine the tinkling of the pianoforte and the fluttering of ladies' fans at a Monday "At Home" in the parlors, for little has changed since the death of "Miss Daisy" Mallory, who lived in the house for eighty-six of her ninety-eight years. After Miss Daisy's death in 1969, her heirs gave the house to the DAR-SAR-CAR, and it is open to the public, a moment frozen in time.

The house was possibly begun in 1852 by Isaac B. Kirtland, who sold it in 1864 to Benjamin Babb, who added the second story before selling it to James Columbus Neely in 1883. Neely had come to Memphis about the time the house was being built, and had formed a partnership with William Goyer in the wholesale grocery business, later going into business with S.

H. Brooks as grocers, cotton factors and commission merchants.

Neely restyled the house again in the 1890s, adding the third floor with its dormers and gables, and heightening the tower to get a view of the river. He enlarged the house to twenty-five rooms, changed the stairway, and installed a stained glass window bought at the Chicago World's Fair. Mr. Neely was said to be the first Memphian to use window screens, and the walls have air channels, providing an early kind of air conditioning.

When Mr. Neely died in 1901, he left the house to his wife Fannie and children. The three sons sold their interest to their sister Frances, called Daisy, who had married Barton Lee Mallory, the son of another cotton factor and grocer, Captain W. B. Mallory, who had moved to Memphis from Virginia.

With the exception of a few years in a New York fin-

ABOVE:
The opulence of the Victorian era has remained unchanged in the drawing room of the Mallory-Neely house.

ishing school and her early childhood in the house on Jefferson Avenue where she was born, Miss Daisy lived at 652 Adams for most of her long life. Because of this single occupancy, the house has remained unchanged. Even the gas lights in the drawing room and music room have never been converted to electricity.

There are elaborately carved cornices and painted ceilings on the first floor. The heavily ornamented and frescoed drawing room ceilings combine geometric shapes, fruit garlands and female masks, executed by Cincinnati craftsmen. The two original marble mantels in the drawing room have been replaced by period carved mahogany etagere mantelpieces with beveled glass mirrors and satyr heads. The music room ceiling design incorporates the names of famous authors: Byron, Longfellow, Milton, Shakespeare, Dickens, and Scott. The dining room retains its tooled leather wainscoting and carved doors and woodwork. The col-

ors are fading now, but the deep red velvet draperies, the gold and silver raised felt wall coverings, the gilded plaster cornices and ceilings, the ornate Empire sofa, the gilded rococo revival pieces, and the prisms and frosted glass of the gas chandeliers speak of opulence and grandeur.

The exterior of the house is dark stucco over brick. A long stone stairway leads up from the front walk to an arcaded porch topped by a balustrade. The center tower has a round-arched entry to the porch on the first floor, a single round-arched window on the second, double windows and a stone balcony on the third, bracketed molding under three arched windows on the fourth story and a four-sided tall peaked roof over all. Dormers and gables and bays, quoined corners and heavy cornices make the house one of the truest depictions of Victorian style in Memphis. It is open to the public under the auspices of the DAR-SAR-CAR. ■

OPPOSITE LEFT:
The Mallory-Neely house at 652 Adams is open to the public.

AT LEFT:
The ceiling of the music room at the Mallory-Neely house incorporates the names of famous authors in its design.

Massey House

1840s

 The oldest house in the neighborhood is the one-story neo-classic clapboard house surrounded by tall trees at 664 Adams. The house was built between 1844 and 1849 by a lawyer named Benjamin Massey. More than a century and a quarter later, the house again belongs to a lawyer who has converted it to offices.

The house has changed hands frequently, but the various owners have maintained its integrity. The owners after the Civil War were James Maydwell and his wife Sophia Harsson Maydwell, whose father had built the first rear section of the house on the corner of Adams and Orleans now known as the James Lee Me-

morial. Tradition has it that Jefferson Davis and his wife were frequent guests of the Maydwells.

The house is clapboard with a neo-classic porch and portico supported by Doric columns. It has floor-length front windows and a wide front doorway with sunburst transom. The one-and-a-half inch thick cypress floors are original. There is a central hall with rooms on both sides. A modern addition houses kitchen and bath at the back.

Set back from the street at the end of a long walk lined with boxwood, and surrounded by magnolias, azaleas, dogwoods and wisteria, the house retains its quaint charm.

ABOVE:
*The Massey house was
built in the 1840s.*

OPPOSITE LEFT:
*Jones and Baldwin
designed the Fontaine
House at 680 Adams in
1870.*

AT LEFT:
*The stairway at the
Fontaine House, which
is open as a museum.*

Fontaine House

1 8 7 0

 The architects Edward Culliatt Jones and Mathias Harvey Baldwin designed both the front addition to 690 Adams and the house next door at 680 Adams, making the corner of Adams and Orleans a monument to their partnership.

Unlike its neighbors, the house at 680 Adams, now known as the Fontaine House, was all built at one time, mostly in 1870, giving it complete design unity. Amos Woodruff commissioned the architects, and the house was completed before mid-1871, in time for the marriage of his daughter Mary Louise, in December, 1871.

Woodruff came to Memphis from Rahway, New Jersey, in 1845, as a maker of buggies and carriages. He became president of two banks, a railroad company, a hotel company, an insurance company, a cotton compress and a lumber firm, as well as alderman and president of the city council. Obviously he needed a house worthy of his status, so he paid $12,600 for the land and $40,000 to erect an imposing residence. Three Woodruff family weddings were held here during the occupancy of Amos Woodruff, his wife and four children, from 1870 to 1883.

The first bride in the house was Woodruff's nineteen-year-old daughter Mollie, who married Egbert Wooldridge on December 18, 1871. The newlyweds lived with her parents in a suite of rooms on the second floor. Their first and only son was born in 1875 and died almost immediately in the bedroom at the rear of the house. A few months later the young husband fell ill on a fishing trip and was brought home to die.

Mollie continued to live as a widow with her parents until 1883, when she married James Henning. Tragedy struck again and their only child died on the day of its birth in 1885. Mollie Woodruff Henning died in 1932, but there are many who say that her ghost lives on in the upstairs back bedroom at 680 Adams.

Times were not always good for Amos Woodruff, and in 1883 he was forced to sell the house at a loss, taking only $40,000 from Noland Fontaine. Fontaine and his wife Virginia had five sons and four daughters. Fontaine was president of Hill, Fontaine & Company, at one time the world's third largest cotton company. The Fontaines lived in the house for forty-six years. Miss Rosa Lee purchased it for the expansion of her art academy next door in 1930.

The Fontaines held legendary entertainments. In 1892, five state governors and more than two thousand guests attended a reception there to celebrate the completion of the first bridge across the Mississippi River below St. Louis. At another lawn party, John Phillip Sousa was guest conductor of the orchestra. Grover Cleveland was entertained there on his visit to Memphis in 1887.

Cleveland came on his honeymoon, arriving on the steamer Kate Adams. A reception in his honor was held at the Gayoso Hotel. The occasion was marred by the fact that the man who introduced Cleveland, Judge H. T. Ellet, slumped over dead on the platform during the President's speech.

The Fontaine house is French Victorian in style, with a colored slate mansard roof, with wrought iron railing, brick with stone-like foundations, quoins and portico. It is three stories high with a five-story tower in the center of the facade. The windows are topped with molded terra cotta lintels. Its dentiled eaves are trimmed with cypress brackets, and cypress is used for most of the woodwork.

To the left of the tower on the first floor is a marble-floored porch with square posts and pierced railings. In the right or eastern bay are double floor-length windows under a peaked gable. Embossed tin was used for the ceilings of the front porch and hall stairwell.

There are twenty rooms, each with fireplace, and a

AT RIGHT:
A place setting of Mrs. Fontaine's silver, crystal and china. The china was made in France for the Memphis Queensware Company.

large basement as well as the three full stories topped with a mansard tower. The interior has central north-south reception halls on all floors; on the first one a drawing room with adjoining music room on the west, and an octagonal dining room on the east. The builders apparently liked the plan of the Kirtland house two doors west, and used the same layout of rooms.

The carved mahogany entrance doors were imported from France, by the Fontaines, and have their original hardware and the initials N and F for Noland Fontaine. An unusual feature for the time is the walk-in closets.

In 1961 the Memphis Chapter of the Association for the Preservation of Tennessee Antiquities (APTA)

presented restoration pledges of $50,000 to the city, and signed a fifty year lease on the house. In 1964 the restored mansion was opened to the public, unfurnished. During restoration a fake interior door, "the door that goes nowhere," was discovered. It was placed for balance on the north wall in the reception hall, with a large outer door and smaller doors on the sides. On "the door that goes nowhere" is the date February 11, 1871, and the signatures of artisans, grainers and carpenters from Canada, itinerant builders who followed the opportunities to practice their crafts.

Gradually, through gifts, the Fontaine House restoration has been completed, and the interior has been furnished, and it is open to the public.　■

Lee-Fontaine Carriage House

 The carriage house behind the Goyer-Lee mansion was built by Charles Wesley Goyer. When Miss Rosa Lee, daughter of James Lee, Jr., purchased the Fontaine House next door to her father's home in 1930, she had the stables behind both houses joined together to provide a larger area for students of the James Lee Academy of Arts.

The Memphis Little Theater had its first permanent home in this building, too. In 1926 the theater groups presented plays here, moving to the Pink Palace basement in 1929.

Presently the Lee-Fontaine Carriage House is a restaurant. ∎

BELOW:
The Gingerbread Playhouse behind the Fontaine House.

Gingerbread Playhouse and Nineteenth Century Dollhouse

 A favorite spot for visitors to Victorian Village is the Gingerbread Playhouse behind the Fontaine House. J. V. Handwerker, a pharmacist, built it in the 1890s for his children at their home on North Thomas. Through the years the little house served as a playhouse, an office, and for a period was a beauty parlor. In 1972 it was to have been demolished, but was saved by the Memphis Board of Realtors, who had it moved to its present location. Its restoration was completed by the APTA in 1975, and it is a favorite spot for bridal photos as well as for visiting children.

An attractive nineteenth century dollhouse nearby dates from 1874, when it was built by John Walsh, president of North Memphis Savings Bank, for his children. It was given to the APTA in 1964 by his granddaughters. ∎

OPPOSITE RIGHT:
*The Goyer-Lee house at
690 Adams is being
restored by the
Association for the
Preservation of
Tennessee Antiquities.*

Goyer-Lee House

1 8 4 8 - 7 3

The house on the northwest corner of Adams and Orleans is now an imposing companion to its ornate neighbors, but it began as a simple two-story farm house, built in 1848 by William Harsson, a native of Baltimore. One of Harsson's daughters, Sophia, married James Maydwell and lived down the street at 664 Adams. A second daughter, Laura, married Charles Wesley Goyer in 1849. Goyer had come to Memphis from Indiana, and he founded a firm dealing in sugar and molasses and also became president of a bank.

In 1852 Goyer bought his father-in-law's house, and expanded it about 1855 to house his growing family. Laura and her father died in 1861, and in 1865 Goyer married her sister Charlotte. By 1871 it was necessary to expand again (Goyer eventually had ten children), and he hired the architectural firm of Jones and Baldwin who had built the handsome house next door. They added the present ornate front, the third floor, and the tower. Goyer died in 1881.

In 1890 Goyer's heirs sold the house to James Lee, Jr., son of riverboat magnate James Lee. James Lee, Jr., had ten children and had outgrown his home farther west on Adams; after moving to 690 the Lees lived there from 1890 to 1925.

Miss Rosa Lee, one of the daughters, used the house to start the James Lee Memorial Academy of Arts in 1925. She donated the house to the City of Memphis in 1929. The next year she purchased the Fontaine house next door and donated that, too, to the city. The Lee and Fontaine stables behind the mansions were joined in 1931 to provide more room for the art students. In 1942 the property became the home of the Memphis Academy of Art, and the Memphis Art Association's Free School moved across the street to Miss Florence McIntyre's Greek Revival home. The APTA signed a lease with the city in 1961 and restoration on the house is continuing.

The house is built of brick, exposed on the foundations, but covered with stucco on the less important areas and sandstone on the front facade. It has a four-story tower with entry under an arch. To the west is a three-story bay with a porch with wrought iron railings wrapping around the corner. To the eastern side is a two-story bowed bay and another porch with paired columns. There are heavy windows and cornice details, elongated roof and tower brackets, and a standing seam terne metal roof.

The bell from the steamer "James Lee" is on the property. ∎

Noland Fontaine, Senior, built the house across Adams Avenue from his own home as a wedding present for his daughter, Mollie, when she married Dr. William Wood Taylor in 1886. The newlyweds lived with her parents until their house was finished in 1890. Mrs. Taylor lived there until her death in 1936.

The house is a two-story red brick structure with ten rooms. There are two gables facing Adams with heavily decorated eaves. A porch with carved posts and decorated railings and a second floor balcony above is painted white to contrast with the dark red brick. There is much terra cotta trim: in the gable, over the windows and in horizontal lines. Over the triple window on the first floor is a terra cotta mask on the keystone. There are stained glass windows and doors.

It is a handsome example of the late Victorian idea that if one kind of decoration is good, two or three kinds will be better. ■

Mollie Fontaine Taylor House

1 8 8 6

AT RIGHT:
Terra cotta and stained glass, two typical Victorian embellishments, at the Mollie Fontaine Taylor house.

OPPOSITE RIGHT:
Noland Fontaine gave this wedding cake house to his daughter Mollie as a wedding present in 1886.

BELOW:
*Lotus leaf capitals on the
columns highlight the
facade of the
Pillow-McIntyre house,
built in 1852 on Adams.*

Pillow-McIntyre

1852

In striking contrast to the towered and ornate Victorian mansions on the street is the Pillow-McIntyre House. It is in two-story Greek Revival style of dignified simplicity. The house is built of brick and stucco, painted pink. Four columns with lotus leaf capitals on fluted piers support a dentiled pediment over the porch. On the first floor there are two long windows with white painted shutters to the east of the recessed entry. On the second story there are three long windows with shutters. Beveled leaded glass in double doors at the entry lead to thirteen rooms with twelve-foot ceilings, parquet floors and six fireplaces. On the west side is a twentieth century addition.

The house was built about 1852 by C. G. Richardson and later owned by J. M. McCombs. In 1873 it was purchased by General Gideon Johnson Pillow. Pillow was given command of the Tennessee Volunteers (from which the state took its nickname) in the Mexican War because of his friendship with President James K. Polk. Both Polk and Pillow came from Maury County in Middle Tennessee, where Pillow had built another handsome Greek Revival home called Clifton Place. Under Pillow's questionable leadership at the Battle of Cerro Gordo, many of the Tennessee troops were killed or wounded. Virtually all the surviving officers blamed Pillow for the debacle, and when they returned they demanded his court martial. A court martial was held and Pillow was cleared of the charges, and went on to serve in the Civil War with questionable merit.

Pillow's second wife did nothing for his reputation either. She married him in 1872, soon after her first husband's death, and proceeded to run up $53,000 worth of debts in a short time.

In 1880 the house was sold to Peter McIntyre, founder of the first glucose refinery in Memphis. He was married to Ella Goyer, daughter of Charles Wesley Goyer, who lived across the street. Their daughter, Miss Florence McIntyre, inherited the house and in 1942 it became the home of the Memphis Art Association's Free School. Classes were taught there until 1963. Recently it has been an interior decorator's office and home, and law offices.

Jefferson Avenue Townhouses

1 8 6 3   a n d   1 8 6 7

Two handsome townhouses stand side by side on the south side of Jefferson Avenue. The house on the west was built in 1863 as a single-family house, but deeds and city directories show that it changed hands frequently as investment and rental property rather than having a long-time family use. Its architect is unknown. It has Italianate features such as double brackets under the eaves and heavy "eyebrows" over the upstairs windows.

The house to the east was designed by Edward C. Jones for attorney William I. Scott between 1867 and 1869. Scott had come to Memphis in 1858 and married Susan, the daughter of banker James Elder. He served in the Confederate Army and was severely wounded at Shiloh. After the war he became a judge of the Chancery Court of Shelby County; then he and his wife moved to St. Louis in 1875, selling the house to Samuel Ridgeley Cruse, treasurer of the Memphis and Charleston Railroad. Cruse's family lived there until the 1950s. His widow was remarried to William D. Sledge, whose granddaughter, the actress Tallulah Bankhead, visited the house as a child.

The house has heavy arched window trim and small regular brackets supporting the cornice and ventilation grills underneath. Both houses have recessed doors topped by square cornices. ∎

Wright Carriage House   1 8 4 0 s

The small house behind the tall brick wall at the corner of Jefferson and Orleans has had three lives. Originally it was a small farm house built in the 1840s. When a larger house was built the brick building was converted into a carriage house. The large home belonged to General Luke E. Wright (1846-1922), who served in the Confederate army and was attorney-general of Shelby County. He was appointed the first Governor-General of the Phillipines, the first United States ambassador to Japan, and was Secretary of War under Theodore Roosevelt.

When the large house was demolished in the 1960s, the bricks were used to build the wall which surrounds the property. The carriage house, a rectangular brick building with a small cupola, has been converted into a residence by Eldridge Wright, great-grandson of Luke E. Wright. ∎

Lowenstein House   1890-91

Elias Lowenstein arrived in Memphis with thirty-five cents in his pocket. The young man from Darmstadt, Germany, landed in New Orleans in 1854 and hastened to Memphis where his two brothers were living. In 1855 the young men went into the dry goods business, opening as B. Lowenstein and Brothers in 1861. The store quickly became one of the leading establishments of the day. It was to Lowenstein's that Mrs. Elizabeth Meriwether went for supplies when she was allowed to cross the picket lines with a list passed by the military authorities in the middle of the Civil War occupation of Memphis.

Their business prospered. By the time Elias Lowenstein died he had become a director of two banks, a cotton mill and an insurance company. He married Babette Wolff of Memphis, who bore him eight children, two of whom died young; five daughters and one son lived to adulthood. But tragedy struck. Babette Lowenstein died in 1887 at the age of forty-six. She never lived in the fine house Mr. Lowenstein erected at the corner of Jefferson and Manassas. In 1890 he built a house of brick, stone and wood for his family, combining the popular building styles.

The house has a limestone foundation and a hipped roof with gables. An Italianate influence may be seen in the square tower with its pyramidal roof over the entrance on the south facade. The tower has a panelled frieze under the cornice, two arched windows on the third story, a round stained glass window on the second and an off-center stone arched opening with keystone over the entrance which is a Richardson Romanesque touch. To the left of the tower is a bay with irregularly placed and shaped windows and a gabled dormer. To the right of the tower is a veranda with wooden lattice work curving around the eastern side of the building.

There is much decorative work of brick and terra cotta on the facade. The effect is one of solidity, but the decoration and the irregularity of windows and arches add a touch of whimsy.

The interior has a central hall plan. At the rear of the entrance hall is an impressive three-story stairwell with stained glass on each landing. The walls have

fleur-de-lis on plaster friezes with ceiling decorations. There are ornate fireplaces, stained glass windows, carved wooden screens over the interior doors, and elaborate gas chandeliers.

Celia Lowenstein Samelson, daughter of Elias Lowenstein, was an active member of the Nineteenth Century Club, and in 1921 she deeded the property to the club to be used as a residence for young working women who had begun to come into Memphis from rural areas to work in factories during the World War. It was staffed by a housemother and a cook, and girls paid board according to their abilities. The housemother enforced a strict set of rules governing social life. By 1929 so many girls needed a place to live that a small porch on the western side was removed and a two-story wing was added.

But times changed. The need for such a chaperoned home declined, and in 1977 the house reverted to the Lowenstein heirs, who intended to use it for quasi-public purposes. In 1979, under the name Lowenstein House, Inc., it became a treatment center for mental health outpatients. ■

ABOVE:
A fireplace with carved overmantel and decorative tiles and a stained glass window in the Lowenstein house.

AT LEFT:
The Bradford-Maydwell house on Poplar, built on the eve of the Civil War.

Bradford-Maydwell   1859

 The dignified restraint of the Federal style is shown in the Bradford-Maydwell house at 648 Poplar. The house was begun as a two-and-a-half story rectangular gabled structure in 1859. The eastern facade, which has remained unchanged, has windows with plain stone lintels and sills, and green louvered shutters.

The house was later altered to include Italianate elements. The main south facade received an added cornice supported by small carved brackets, and segmentally arched windows on the first floor. The entrance has a round-arched opening with sandstone molding topped by a keystone trimmed with an acanthus leaf.

Recessed in the opening is an arched double front door bordered by rope carving. The upper portions of the doors are glass, while the bottom has carved medallions.

The house has a side hall plan, with a tall staircase and turned balustrades along the western wall of the hall. To the east of the hall are two parlors, each sixteen feet square, with ornate Victorian detail.

W.C. Bradford acquired the lot in 1853 and by 1859 the city directory records a residence there. In 1860 James Maydwell acquired the land, which he subdivided in 1867. The house was probably built in 1859 or 1860 by one of these two men. It has been remodelled as a restaurant. ∎

AT RIGHT:
The Patton house on busy Poplar Avenue was away from the town of Memphis when it was built in 1884.

Patton House 1884

Fire, vandalism, murder and a variety of uses — as a home, an antique shop, a private club, and a restaurant — mark the history of the house at 1085 Poplar, a history belied by its gracious Victorian exterior.

The house was built in 1877 as a plantation house away from the center of Memphis. A fire damaged it in 1883, and in 1884 it was rebuilt using the same bricks. Its owner was Thomas Newton Patton. Patton was born in McLemoresville, Carroll County, Tennesse, in 1831. He enlisted in General Nathan Bedford Forrest's cavalry during the Civil War. Since horses were scarce during the war, each soldier was required to furnish his own. Patton's cousin, J.L. Burne, had a good strong horse hidden from the Yankees in the woods. Burne would only sell the horse if Patton promised to return it after the war. Patton bought the horse, served under Forrest, and managed to return the horse in good condition when the war was over.

After the war Patton moved to Memphis to work for his uncle in a barge and transport company. He married Mollie Terry and lived in the house on Poplar Pike, with their only son. Mollie died of the measles, and sixteen years later Patton married Helen Coulter, and had three more children. Their daughter, Mattie, married General Forrest's grandson in 1905.

In 1900 the Pattons sold the house to Samuel Bejach, a Russian who became a merchant in Memphis, and whose son, L.D. Bejach, became a judge and a state legislator. After the Bejachs, the house had a succession of owners and uses. In 1965 the owner, proprietor of a private club in the house, was murdered on the property. At present, the house is used as a restaurant, and while the interior is much altered, the approach, under tall magnolias, has a touch of its original grace.

The house is built of red brick with nineteen-inch-thick walls, so sturdy that no cracks have appeared. There are two stories with a two-and-a-half story cross gable on the eastern end. There are four exterior chimneys, a low-pitched metal roof, cast iron ventilation grills in the attic and foundation, and a wooden cornice with dentil molding and scrolled brackets. The windows are set in arched openings with brick lintels.

The house is unusual in its front porch and french windows leading to the porch and balcony. No other early house in the city retains these touches, reminiscent of New Orleans. The brick porch, added at the turn of the century, has a wrought iron railing and delicate paired wrought iron columns supporting a second-floor balcony with railing. ∎

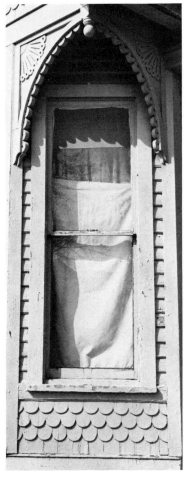

. GREENLAW .

One of the oldest neighborhoods in Memphis, Greenlaw has lived through wars, floods, fevers and urban decay. Two brothers from Virginia, J. Oliver Greenlaw and William Borden Greenlaw, began purchasing land north of Gayoso Bayou in 1849, when North Memphis was the heart of town. In 1856 they laid out the first addition to the original city plan, a thirty-block area bounded on the north by Kerr, on the south by the bayou, on the east by Auction and on the west by North Main. They planned broad cobblestone streets lined with sycamore trees and herringbone brick sidewalks with granite curbs. Some prosperous Memphians bought land for summer retreats, but others built substantial permanent houses.

After the Civil War the area grew as largely working-class people — mechanics, butchers, grocers, a wagon-maker, carpenters — moved in and built modest cottages. For some reason the neighborhood attracted people from the north while areas on the south of town were where people from the neighboring southern states settled. In 1867 a bridge across Gayoso Bayou at Front Street made the area even more accessible, and by 1869 it was considered part of Chelsea. In the second half of the nineteenth century Greenlaw had a great ethnic diversity; Germans, Jews, Irish, and blacks all lived there.

Greenlaw had its heyday around the turn of the century when many families still active in Memphis today lived there. Gradually the neighborhood has fallen into decay, but the charm of its Victorian cottages remains.

Porter-Leath
Children's Center

1 8 5 6 - 1 9 2 0 s

The six structures that make up the Porter-Leath Children's Center were built over a period of years from 1856 to the 1920s. Throughout that time and down to the present, Porter-Leath has provided shelter, comfort and care for children in need.

In 1850 the Protestant Widows and Orphans Asylum was first chartered. In 1854 it came to use the present location when Mrs. Sarah Leath donated nine acres of land on New Raleigh Road (now Chelsea). A public subscription was begun, and the first building was completed in 1856 — a brick, two-story structure with a hipped roof and cast iron capped rectangular windows. This was the home for seven boys, seven girls and a matron. When Mrs. Leath died in 1858, she left an additional twenty acres to the orphanage, and directed that her slaves were to be sold to provide operating funds. The name was changed to the Leath Orphan Asylum.

Adjoining the original building to the south is a much larger three-story brick building which was added in 1875. The Independent Order of Odd Fellows raised the money for its construction, and it was designed by prominent architect Edward Culliatt Jones. In the front (west) side of the building is a three-story bay window whose second-story cornice bears the legend "Leath Orphanage, Erected 1.0.0. F. 1875." Each of the three stories of the building is marked by brick cornice work with elaborate brick piers. The windows are topped by segmental arches with keystones. On either side of the bay are porches; ornate brackets support the roof cornice.

Dr. D. T. Porter, whose many civic activities included an interest in the orphanage, added his name to it in 1904. His daughter gave a gift of $103,000 in his memory, and the name was changed to Porter Home and Leath Orphanage. In 1951 it became the Porter-Leath Home.

Many other prominent citizens and organizations supported the orphanage and new additions were made to it in 1912, 1927 and 1929. The 1927 building, a two-story white stucco with tiled roof at the southern end of the complex, was named Gould Cottage for its donor, a New York millionaire named Edwin Gould. Once while Gould was changing trains in Memphis, he loaded a taxi with dime store toys and went to see the superintendent of the Orphanage, whom he had known in Arkansas. His visit resulted in a gift of $50,000.

C. W. Goyer, who lived in the Goyer-Lee mansion at the corner of Adams and Orleans, was a member of the Odd Fellows and president of the Orphanage board for many years. Sometimes Goyer would get up before dawn, walk from his home to the Orphanage, do several hours of work there, then go to his desk downtown for a regular day.

As attitudes and needs changed, so did the services offered by Porter-Leath. Today dependent, neglected and abused children are sheltered in foster homes under the supervision of Porter-Leath, and an emergency center, a family day-care program, an after-school program and medical services keep the old building alive, still serving children in need.

■

Harris Memorial Methodist Church 1898

Harris Memorial Methodist Church is an example of a Victorian neighborhood church. Built in Greenlaw in 1898, it replaced a frame structure on Saffarans Street that the congregation had used since 1864. The church was named for Dr. George W. D. Harris, who led a hectic debate to organize the Methodist Memphis Conference.

Although the architect is unknown, the church follows the "Akron Plan" also used in First Methodist downtown. It is a red brick building with white stone trim and pointed arch doorways. There is a corner steeple tower and a spireless tower to its left. The sanctuary features a peaked ceiling and a cross shaped plan. The Cathedral Art Glass Windows depict Biblical scenes. It is an example of the late nineteenth century toning down of ornamentation with emphasis on balance and simplified interiors. ■

AT RIGHT:
Harris Memorial Methodist Church at 602 Looney.

George C. Love House 1889

The George Collins Love house has two areas of significance: its architecture, which is typical of middle class residences at the end of the nineteenth century, and its association with the politics of the Crump era in the early twentieth century.

George Love arrived in Memphis in 1862, from Indiana, and after several business ventures, found success in making white oak barrel staves and shipping them to Europe and the cities of the United States. When he became chairman of the Board of Public Works, he had charge of streets, bridges and sewers and established a political friendship with Edward Hull Crump that was to continue as Crump solidified his power in Memphis.

In 1915 Crump ran for re-election as mayor. His election was disputed by opponents who filed a suit in court to oust Crump. Since Crump could not legally assume the office until the suit was settled, he used his influence to have the city council appoint Love as an interim mayor. Love served as "caretaker" mayor from November 4, 1915, till February 12, 1916, when Crump, having cleared his legal difficulties, took office. Love lived in this house till his death in 1928.

At one time there must have been many houses in the neighborhood like the Love house in appearance and character; however, only this one has survived intact. Love's daughters, Mary and Octavia, lived in the house until 1976 when it was given to the city.

The house is located at the eastern boundary of the Greenlaw subdivision, which was developed in 1856, the first subdivision laid out after the original city plan. For a time the home was surrounded by peach orchards and a small farm, and when it was built by Love in 1889, it was intended as country retreat and summer cottage on the road to Raleigh.

The house has two stories and fourteen rooms. A brick foundation with arched vents covered with cast iron grills supports the white frame house. A skirt of vertical siding divides the first and second floors; diagonal shiplap siding appears on the front gable. A side gable is ornamented with latticed, pierced siding, a decoration that appears on many houses in the neighborhood. Across the first floor is a wooden front porch with lathe-turned posts and balustrade. There is dentil molding above the windows and front door and at the porch cornice.

The interior still has its original mantels, both wooden and cast iron, shutters at the windows, brass carpet runners on the stairs, and brass doorknobs and latches.

The entrance hall is on the north side with a staircase on its back wall. To the left of the hall are two formal parlors and a small office. Behind the entrance hall is the dining room, with an unusual treatment of walls and ceiling, diagonally grooved cedar panelling. Doorways have interior transoms. Upstairs are four bedrooms and a central hall.

An original white wrought iron fence borders the front of the property. ∎

BELOW:
Diagonally grooved cedar panelling covers all the surfaces in the dining room of the Love house.

OPPOSITE RIGHT:
Now owned by the city, the Love house at 619 N. Seventh is an example of a comfortable, middle-class residence of the late nineteenth century.

1 8 9 0

Artesian Water Pumping Station

 The modern city of Memphis began with the calamities of the 1870s. The disastrous yellow fever epidemics not only decimated the population but called into question the efficiency of civic organization.

Until 1870 Memphis relied on cisterns, springs and shallow wells, often located near privies, with little concern for sanitation. When the Memphis Water Company was organized that year, the chief worry was not drinking water, but water for fighting fires. By 1873 the company had erected a pumping station on the south bank of the Wolf River, signed a contract with the city for fire hydrants, and laid seventeen miles of pipes.

Then came the three epidemics of the 1870s. The disease reached its peak in September, 1878, when people were dying at the rate of two hundred a day. The coming of frost on October 18 that year meant the end of that summer's plague, but by that time the city was bankrupt. In January, 1879, the city charter was revoked and the city was to remain a Taxing District till 1893.

The cause of yellow fever was a mystery, but the sorry state of the city was recognized. The first steps of the leaders of the Taxing District were to organize a more powerful Board of Health. A new Waring sewage system meant that, by 1900, fifty-two miles of sewers were in operation. The condition of the streets was a concern; ninety-five miles of new hard pavement was begun.

One of the greatest changes came about in 1887. Richard Graves of the Bohlen-Huse Ice Company contracted to dig a deep well on their property at Court Avenue and Gayoso Bayou; suddenly Memphis discovered that it was sitting on pure water in an aquifer deep underground. The Artesian Water Company, under President J.G. Latham, began the drilling of forty wells. But the progress was too slow and the prices were too high, and in 1903 the city purchased the utility and began to improve services and lower prices. Pure, cheap water became one of the city's greatest assets.

The permanent pumping plant was considered a daring and successful engineering achievement when it began operating in 1890. About eighty-five feet below the surface a tunnel was constructed in a stratum of firm clay. Brick-lined tunnels five feet in diameter supplied water from forty-two wells into a reservoir of two million gallons.

The building built to house this marvel is dark red brick with white stone horizontal elements. On the north facade is a stepped gable with crenelations on the gable and the side bays. A row of decorated tile arches is under the crenelations. An arched double window centers the gable over an arched entryway. ■

Burkle House   1849

When Jacob Burkle built his house in 1849, it was in the country. The only way to reach Memphis was to travel east to near the site of today's St. Joseph Hospital and cross Gayoso Bayou. His house faced Old Randolph Road, now North Second Street.

Jacob Burkle came to the United States with his brother and sister from Schmeden, near Stuttgart, Germany. He made the decision to leave Germany because he feared conscription into Bismarck's army. Soon after their arrival his sister Rosina married another immigrant, Jacob Buerer, and the families settled near each other.

Jacob Burkle's house was convenient to the stockyard which he owned and in which several members of the family worked. The stockyard was east of the house, stretching from Chelsea to Bickford. South of the house was a tavern, also owned by the family, which catered to drovers of hogs, turkeys and geese. Behind the house was a kiln and brickyard. The backyard was paved in a herringbone pattern of broken bricks that could not be sold.

Jacob married twice, once to Maria Rebecca Vorwerk, who came from Bremen. His second wife was much younger. His descendants lived in the house until the late 1970s. The original Burkle's Bakery was nearby at the corner of North Second and Bickford.

The house is a one-story frame house with a central hall. In 1859 rooms were added in an ell in the rear and a small porch with square pillars was added over the entrance. There are brick gutters which carried water into a cistern. The interior woodwork is pine or cypress and was painted with a fake wood grain in the nineteenth century. ■

ABOVE:
This 1849 cottage on North Second was built for Jacob Burkle, one of many German residents of Memphis.

VANCE-PONTOTOC

 The "Kid Glove Section" was the name given to the Vance-Pontotoc area in its heyday in the 1880s. There was an aristocratic air about the tree-lined cobblestone streets whose residents were bankers, attorneys, cotton brokers, carriage makers, and steamboat captains — recipients of the burgeoning prosperity of Memphis in the two decades after the worst yellow fever outbreaks.

Citizens with names like Goodbar, Hayes, Barton, Heiskell and Woodson built fine houses in many styles: Italianate town houses and Queen Anne mansions intermingling with more modest Victorian frame dwellings.

Today the area bounded by Pontotoc, Cynthia, Vance and Danny Thomas is a sad victim of urban decay. But remnants of the architectural grandeur that developed between 1858 and 1918 remain. Ornamental woodwork above doorways and around lathe-turned columns and balustrades, pressed tin decoration, jigsaw brackets, cast iron ornaments and leaded glass all give hints of former glory. ∎

ADDITIONAL MEMPHIS ARCHITECTURE

Elmwood Cemetary

 In the midst of busy railroads and highways lies Elmwood Cemetery, silent city within a city, burial place for over 70,000 Memphians. The visitor who strolls over the rolling grounds under tall trees can contemplate the lives of the famous and the obscure, the lives that made Memphis' history.

Elmwood was founded in 1852 when fifty citizens subscribed $500 apiece to form an association and buy forty acres, then two miles beyond the city limits. In February, 1854, a charter was obtained from the state of Tennessee and amended in 1873, making it the only cemetery chartered by the state legislature.

In 1856, it advertised in the *Appeal*:

> Elmwood Cemetery, beautifully situated about two miles south-east from Memphis, has reduced the price of lots to a uniform rate of 25¢ a square foot. Terms cash, or note for four months with good endorser, payable at bank, without interest.

The name "Elmwood" was drawn from a hat full of suggested names in 1852. The beauty of the place always attracted visitors. In June, 1874, the *Appeal* said, "The officers of Elmwood Cemetery announce that they will buy two dozen young squirrels for the cemetery. Apply at the office at 36 Union Street, Memphis." Rules had to be made. From a 1928 list of cemetery regulations:

> Persons on horseback, in carriages or automobiles will not be allowed to leave the drives, or pass through the grounds at a speed exceeding eight miles an hour.
>
> No person with dogs, firearms or refreshments will be permitted to enter the cemetery.
>
> No children will be admitted unless accompanied by some adult person responsible for their conduct.

The cemetery is entered over a high arched bridge built in 1903 over the railroad tracks. On the left after the entrance is the office, a Gothic cottage, with carved bargeboards. There is a bell tower over a brick vault where cemetery records are kept. The bell has been here since the late 1800s and used to be tolled each time a funeral procession entered the grounds.

The office interior has panelled wainscoting, a large walnut desk counter and a fireplace with solid oak mantel.

There are twenty-two mayors of Memphis and South Memphis buried in Elmwood, including E.H. "Boss" Crump, who "wouldn't 'low no easy riding" and wielded absolute power in the first half of the twentieth century; William Spickernagle, who led a reform ticket and cleaned up the flatboat traffic in the 1840s; David Park "Pappy" Hadden, who invented "Hadden's horn," a device insuring the honesty of dice games; and Dr. D. T. Porter, who helped clean up the city after the yellow fever epidemic of the 1870s.

Two governors of Tennessee are buried there: Isham Green Harris, who was in office when the Civil War broke out, and James C. Jones, known as "Lean Jimmy" Jones, who defeated James K. Polk for governor. There are also the graves of four United States senators.

Elmwood is perhaps best known as a resting place for Confederate soldiers. There are many buried there, including seventeen Rebel generals and one lone Yankee general. But the rest has not been final for some. Nathan Bedford Forrest was buried in Elmwood until his remains were removed to Forrest Park on Union in 1905. Two sons of Jefferson Davis, president of the Confederacy, were buried there, but their graves were removed in 1895.

The only marked grave of a Revolutionary War soldier lies with veterans of the War of 1812. There are graves of pioneers, patriots and patriarchs.

Dorothea Spottswood Henry Winston, daughter of Patrick Henry, was buried there in 1854. William Person, who planted the first cotton seed in Shelby County; Professor Herman Frank Arnold, who orchestrated the tune which became famous as "Dixie" and played it at Jefferson Davis' inauguration; Ginny Moon, Confederate spy; Kit Dalton of the Jesse James gang; Robert Church, Senior, Memphis' first black millionaire; Elder Blair T. Hunt, noted black educator, — these are some of the well-known names in Elmwood.

A reminder of Memphis' great tragedies is the number of graves dating from the yellow fever epidemics of 1873 and 1878. Annie Cook, a prostitute who turned her bordello into a hospital and died nursing the victims, lies near six Episcopal nuns of St. Mary's who gave their lives in the epidemic.

The saints and sinners who made Memphis, lie under the tall trees in the quiet of Elmwood. ■

Coward Place

1843-56

One of the busiest and most famous ante-bellum homes in Memphis is the old Coward Place, which, since 1958, has been Justine's, an award-winning restaurant.

The site, "thirteen poles from the Memphis and La-Grange Railroad . . . near a black walnut tree," was originally part of the Ramsey grant. Nathaniel Ragland bought two hundred and fifty-two acres in 1838 and sold three acres of it to Mrs. Mildred Anderson in 1843. Mrs. Anderson built a house on her property, and in 1856 sold it for $3,000 to Hosea Merrill Grosvenor who owned the adjoining farm as well as two furniture stores in Memphis.

Grosvenor enlarged the house, apparently inspired by the French Colonial architecture he had seen in New Orleans. The walls are eighteen inches thick hand-made brick and the front facade is covered with a stucco-like finish made from mixing brick dust, red sand and baked crushed limestone. The original soft pink color was found under fourteen layers of later paint.

The interior has a central hall with double parlors on each side with fourteen-foot ceilings and original marble mantels. Many old items have been used in the present decoration: carved oak doors from a house that stood at Vance and Wellington, a balustrade and marble from the old Gayoso Hotel, wrought iron gates from an old synagogue in Louisiana and stones in the patio from the Jefferson Davis house on Court.

During the Civil War a skirmish was fought on the lawn. Union soldiers were quartered in the house with the Grosvenor family. Descendants say that Grosvenor was killed by a Yankee officer as he tried to get help for his wife, who was dying in childbirth. Two children survived the tragedy and were raised by relatives. The house was sold in 1866 but a portion of the original farm still belongs to the Grosvenor family.

The new owner was attorney William Coward, who gave the house as a wedding present to his son Samuel in 1872 when he married Ida Carroll, the daughter of Major General William Carroll, a hero of the Battle of New Orleans and governor of Tennessee. Between 1866 and 1879 the house was probably used as a country retreat, and it was not until 1879 that Samuel and Ida Coward moved there. Family tradition says that the Carroll family in Memphis "wept to see Ida going so far away."

By 1889 the city had grown so that the limits were extended to include the house. The Cowards' only child, Elizabeth, married Richard O. Johnston in 1901 and they moved in. A large Victorian front porch was added, the house was painted battleship gray, and small wings were added on the west and south. In the 1920s Mrs. Johnston divided the house into apartments. After her death in 1952 the house fell into disrepair as the neighborhood around it became industrial and commercial.

The house became a restaurant in 1956 and restoration was begun. The front porch was removed and pegs, indicating a smaller porch had surmounted the entrance, were found. The paint was scraped away and eight windows on the front were repaired to match the one original cornice remaining. The white marble steps now at the entrance were found buried in the yard. The front facade is topped by a simple cornice supported by curved brackets. Circular cast iron ventilation grills are above each of the five second-story windows.

Now diners at Justine's can enjoy a gracious nineteenth century atmosphere.

ABOVE:
The Coward Place, built before the Civil War, now houses Justine's Restaurant.

AT RIGHT:
Annesdale, built in 1855,was used as a hospital for victims of Shiloh.

Annesdale

1 8 5 5

October 14, 1903 was a day to remember. From the Peabody Hotel where luncheon was served, fifteen wagons filled with watermelons followed trolley cars jammed with people out to an area just east of the city. As Arnold's brass band played and melons were split, the sale of lots commenced. When the proceedings were over, 40 Memphians had spent $71,000 to purchase land in Annesdale Park, the South's first subdivision. P.T. Barnum couldn't have done it better. But the enduring history of Annesdale Park has proven those initial buyers were not Barnum's kind of suckers.

— From a pamphlet, "Midtown"

The Annesdale-Snowden District is an urban success story. The neighborhood and the Snowden family are entertwined. The story goes back to the mid-1850s, when Dr. Samuel Mansfield, a wholesale druggist from Maryland, built an elegant Italianate mansion on a knoll overlooking Pigeon Roost Road (now Lamar Avenue). During the Civil War, the mansion was converted into a hospital where victims of the Battle of Shiloh, one hundred miles away, were sent.

In 1869, Colonel Robert C. Brinkley purchased the house and two hundred acres as a wedding gift for his daughter Annie Overton Brinkley (a granddaughter of Memphis founder John Overton) and her husband Colonel Robert Bogardus Snowden. Both Brinkley and Snowden were men of vision who had much to do with the development of Memphis. Colonel Brinkley was one of the original backers of the first railroad to come to Memphis. He also attracted the interest of financier George Peabody, who invested in Memphis without ever visiting it. Brinkley secured Peabody's investment capital, and named a major street, a school, a park, and a famous hotel (eventually owned by Brinkley's daughter Annie) after him.

Colonel Snowden was born in New York of Dutch ancestry, but came to Tennessee at the age of three. He served under General Johnston at Shiloh, and after the war he became a liquor merchant. He married Annie Overton Brinkley in 1869 and moved into the mansion, christened Annesdale in the bride's honor. During the yellow fever epidemics of 1873 and 1878, Colonel Snowden remained in Memphis and bought as much land as he could acquire, the basis for future development. He became president of the Bank of Commerce and the Citizen's Electric Street Railway before his death in 1909.

Today the Annesdale Mansion sits on a seven-and-a-half acre hilltop bounded on three sides by Snowden Circle and on the north by Lamar. The house is surrounded by tall trees and dense shrubbery. Its park-like setting has frequently been mistaken for a lovers' lane and once a dead body was found under a magnolia tree.

The house is an Italian-style villa built of bricks hand-fired on the place in 1855. The front, or north, facade has a tower reaching two stories above the terra cotta tiled hip roof. The first floor of the tower is reached by stone steps to a single arched opening to the entry and porch. On the second floor of the tower is a single square window and a bracketed balcony. On the third level are two round-arched windows and on the fourth are four narrow round-arched windows on each side, the whole topped by a low-pitched tile roof bracketed at the eaves.

On the eastern side of the house is a two-story sun porch added in 1900. It has arched french windows on the first floor and square linteled windows on the second. Between the sunporch and the tower, a square-gabled bay extends beyond the facade, with a round-arched bay window on the first floor and a balcony under arched windows on the second. The gable has large brackets supporting the eaves and a circular attic window under the pediment.

West of the tower and slightly recessed is another bay. A round-arched arcade porch extends around the corner and across the west side to a porte-cochere. The porch roof forms a balcony to the second floor, which has two round-arched windows and a bracketed hip roof. The corners of the house are quoined, and a two-story wrought iron porch and balcony are at the south, or rear, elevation.

The first floor has ten major rooms with fourteen foot ceilings. A nine foot doorway under a semi-circular transom leads from the entry portion of the porch to the hall, both of which have black and white checked marble floors.

The entry and stair hall portions are separated by a segmentally arched spandrel at the ceiling. Arched doorways lead to the library on the west and the parlor on the east, and at the rear of the hall arched double doors lead to the service hall and back stairs. The staircase is free-standing curving walnut with a crystal newel finial.

The library has an Italian white marble mantel and heavy crown moldings. Behind it is the dining room, with gum panelling surmounted by wallpaper on the top third of the wall. The ceiling has heavy oak beams and joists. On the south wall is a marble-topped serving table on ornate console brackets.

To the east of the entry are the front parlor and music room, which open on to the sun porch. The walls are panelled with a grape carved cornice, and the arabesque painted ceilings have plaster moldings.

The second floor contains a central hall flanked by five bedrooms and baths. The ceilings on this floor are twelve feet, and most of the rooms contain fireplaces with marble mantels. Above the main stairway is a round, patterned, lead set skylight.

Many of the furnishings, light fixtures and draperies are original as the same family has lived in the house for several generations. Colonel Snowden's portrait in the library shows his Civil War saber, which is used by family members to cut their wedding cakes. Colonel Snowden and his wife had three daughters and two

sons, and adopted three cousins, the Tracy girls, making a large family of many ages living in the house in the late nineteenth century.

Family members, including Roberta Galloway Snowden and Thomas Hardy Todd, Jr., report having been awakened shortly after moving into the house by the sound of footsteps coming slowly up the back staircase. When Mrs. Snowden asked her mother-in-law, Annie Overton Brinkley Snowden, if the footsteps could be Colonel Snowden's ghost, Mother Snowden replied, "Colonel Snowden *never* used the back stairs."

The house and grounds have been the scene of many elegant entertainments from a *Fête Champêtre* soon after the Snowdens moved in 1869 down to weddings of the present day. Delicacies served have included mushrooms grown in the brick basement and oysters fattened in barrels in the cellars.

The present resident, May Snowden Todd, remembers a circus parade staged as a practical joke by friends of her father, John Bayard Snowden. A circus was unloading its animals in a nearby train yard at one a.m. The friends rerouted the whole parade of animals so that they marched around the spacious Annesdale grounds.

Colonel Snowden's sons, John Bayard Snowden and Robert Brinkley Snowden, became partners in real estate development, and in 1903 developed what is called "the first subdivision in the south," Annesdale Park. It began with fanfare worthy of Barnum and featured all the modern conveniences to attract affluent Memphians: gas street lights, sewers and gas and water mains. Its success was immediate, and in 1906, the Snowden brothers developed South Annesdale. By 1910 the original farm had been broken down and the streets running through it were named for the Snowden children: Dorothy, Bayard (now Central) and Brinkley (now Sledge).

The new owners of the lots were leading members of the community: doctors, bankers, insurance men and levee contracters. The homes they built provide a record of the building styles popular between 1903 and 1929. One or one-and-a-half story houses with a veranda, bungalows of weatherboard or brick, and four square style houses dominate the area. Building elements frequently seen include large porches, tapered columns, dormers, both hip and gable roofs, many with jerkin-heads. Materials are stone, stucco, shingles and concrete block as well as brick and board. Many houses are decorated by bracketed cornices, bay windows, transoms and sidelights, leaded and stained glass windows and porte cocheres. The houses are set back from the street thirty-five feet on lots that are typically fifty feet by one hundred feet.

The housing shortage of the 1940s and the eastward sprawl of the city in the '50s and '60s meant decline to Annesdale Park and many of the houses were subdivided from single family use. But the location, the mature trees and the structural soundness of the

houses have combined to reverse that trend. In 1975 the Annesdale-Snowden Neighborhood Association was formed to halt further commercial encroachment and to improve the neighborhood. A comprehensive neighborhood plan was adopted, resulting in down zoning to the original single family designation. Historic district status was granted the area bounded by I-255 to the west, Heistan Place to the south and Lamar on the north and east. New confidence, pride and stability characterize the neighborhood today, making it the success story of neighbors appreciating the heritage of the neighborhood. ∎

ABOVE:
Painted ceiling in the parlor of Annesdale.

OPPOSITE LEFT:
The breakfast room at Annesdale.

BELOW:
Wrought iron porches on the south of Annesdale.

Ashlar Hall

1896

Another Snowden home is a landmark in the area immediately northeast of Annesdale. Ashlar Hall, a gray limestone castle located in the triangle of Central Avenue, Lamar Avenue and Melrose Street, has fascinated passers-by for years and is now used as a restaurant.

The builder was one of the two sons of Colonel and Mrs. Snowden of Annesdale, Robert Brinkley Snowden (1869-1942). He graduated from Princeton in 1890 and returned to Memphis to become first a real estate developer in partnership with his brother and later a banker. He had studied architecture at Princeton, and he designed a house for himself to be set on seven acres near his parents' home, on wooded land where as a boy he had hunted quail, possum, coons and rabbits.

The fortress-like house is built of Indiana hewn limestone, or "ashlar," from which it takes its name. The stone was delivered to Memphis on barges and set in place by masons from Nashville. It cost $24,900 when it was built in 1896, and Mr. Snowden designed every detail from the gargoyles to the floor plan. The house has eight rooms on two main floors, plus an attic and a basement which housed his admirable wine cellar. Italian craftsmen executed the stained glass windows in the stairwell and the oak carvings on the foyer mantel.

Irregularity of form and massiveness mark the exterior of Ashlar Hall. There is a major tower on the southwest and three smaller towers, all topped with stone battlements. Tall chimneys rise above the towers. Stone porch railings with circular cut-outs curve around the north, east and west sides. There is a porte cochere with round columns having foliated capitals with faces in the design. Gargoyles leap from cornices and walls randomly, ejecting water from roof and parapet. ∎

AT RIGHT:
Ashlar Hall, designed by Robert Brinkley Snowden in 1896.

AT LEFT:
*The Rozelle house, built
in the 1850s, is in the
heart of Midtown.*

Rozelle House

1850s

 Solomon Rozelle settled in Shelby County before Memphis was even planned. Today the house that his descendants built stands in Midtown, a gracious reminder of early times.

Solomon Rozelle was born in Baltimore in 1777, the son of French Huegenots. He moved first to Maury County, Tennessee, then in 1815 moved west again, acquiring some sixteen hundred acres of virgin land in Shelby County, the boundaries of which were present-day East Parkway, Cane Creek on the south, Bellevue on the west and part of Union Avenue on the north. The land was a wildernes of red oak, poplar, red gum, walnut and cherry trees when Rozelle, his family and his slaves set out to clear it. His slaves were said to be the first Negroes in Shelby County. His youngest son, Blackmon, was the first white child born west of the Tennessee River in Tennessee.

Rozelle, Tillman Bettis and Anderson Carr were the first permanent white settlers in the area, and they set themselves up as the first county court before the town was laid out in 1819. Rozelle's house, built on the highest ground near what became the intersection of Pidgeon Roost Road (Lamar) and the Memphis & Charleston Railroad tracks, was the stopping place for Methodist Circuit riders who began to come to the new settlement, and he, his wife, two sons and a son-in-law were among the eleven incorporators of the First Methodist Church in 1826. Rozelle donated a parcel of land which was sold to provide funds for the first church building.

The area was growing fast. In 1840, thirty-five years after his arrival in the wilderness, Rozelle donated a right-of-way down the two-mile length of his property to the first railroad, and a station along the line was named for him. He died in 1856, aged seventy-nine, survived by his wife Mary and several children. His children inherited the property and in 1853 C. W. Rozelle is shown as owning thirty acres of today's Central Gardens district. The white frame house on Harbert was built about that time.

The house is built of yellow poplar siding and tapered shingles. There are six gables, the two largest forming the front of the house. There is a double doorway with an overhead fanlight and side glass panels in the right front gable and a double window in the left. Double windows center each front gable in the second story. Dentil molding and intricate carving ornament the exterior. A wide foyer with wide plank floors, living and dining rooms to the left, and stairs to the right mark the interior.

■

1856

Rayner House

 Eli Rayner was born in North Carolina in 1815 and moved as a young man to Fayette County, Tennessee. He married May Jones, of a prominent Memphis family, and became a prosperous planter, encouraging his relatives back in North Carolina to join him in western Tennessee. He was a scientific farmer, and in 1851 one of his bales of cotton was exhibited at the London Industrial Exhibition — a perfect bale weighing five hundred pounds and remarkable for its fineness, softness, whiteness and beauty. The *Memphis Daily Appeal* of January 7, 1851, boasted, "It will be magnificent proof of the productiveness of the cotton region in the most favored positions, and will be useful to give an idea as to what our transatlantic rivals have to compete with in their efforts to grow cotton in India and the West Indies."

In 1856 Rayner moved his family, two daughters and three sons, closer to the cultural and educational opportunities of Memphis, purchasing two thousand acres of prime cotton land along the route of the as-yet-unfinished Memphis and Charleston Railroad. Here he built his house and laid out extensive vegetable and flower gardens and even greenhouses where he grew lemons and oranges.

The two-story frame house, underpinned with yellow poplar, shows the hand of a designer familiar with details of the Greek Revival style and possessing a considerable aesthetic awareness. The floor plan is a typical center hall design. The three parlors are separated by large sliding doors, called "pocket doors." The house once faced south, but was turned on logs to face west when Rayner subdivided the property before his death in 1892. At one time the house had several outbuildings, including a "garçoniere," a separate living area for the sons of the family and their tutor. At some time, possibly when the house was turned, one wing was separated from the main house and moved to the corner of Willett and Southern.

The facade, which now faces west, has tall fluted wooden columns with cast-metal lotus leaf capitals. Above these in the two-story central section is a handsome pediment supported by scrolled brackets. A cast iron balcony on the second story extends the width of the portico. One-story wings flank the central portico with floor-to-ceiling double-hung windows with movable shutters. The entrance has a leaded glass transom and sidelights. The millwork throughout reflects a simple Greek key motif.

Twice the grove of trees around the house became a campground. During the Civil War, Union troops were posted there to protect the roadbed of the railroad from Confederate marauders. Tradition says that Rayner hid his wife's jewelry in the greenhouse, where it was found by accident and stolen by Yankee soldiers.

In the 1878 yellow fever epidemic the grove again became a campground, this time for refugees from the fever, sent there by the Howard Society.

One of Rayner's daughters, Louisa, married Dr. W. R. Hodges, who died of yellow fever in the epidemic. Another daughter, Irene, married Thomas Battle Turley, who became senator from Tennessee. Eli Rayner, Jr., had a reputation as a woman chaser and spent much of his time in New York pursuing actresses. Juan, at seventeen, rode with Nathan Bedford Forrest's cavalry, and is said to have been one of the troopers who rode into the Chisca Hotel in an attempt to capture a Union general. ∎

AT LEFT:
The grove around Eli Rayner's Greek Revival house was a campground for Federal troops in the Civil War and again in the 1870s for refugees from yellow fever.

Elam House

1 8 5 4

 The only surviving nineteenth-century log building in Memphis is the Elam Homestead. Although several additions have been made through the years, the original portion of the building shows early log construction techniques.

The house was built by Edward Simpson Elam sometime before 1854. The land on which it stands was originally part of a land grant made in 1791 to John Lynch for his service in the Revolutionary War and included the area from Prescott to Lamar and from Kimball to Nonconnah Creek. In 1821 Lynch's heirs sold the land to J. Kimble. His heirs started selling off tracts, and Elam bought 444¼ acres from Kimble in 1849 for $3,620.

Edward Elam and his brother John Simpson Elam were among the first settlers in this area, coming here from Virginia. John Elam obtained two thousand acres from the Chickasaw Indians. John's land was south of Edward's in the Whitehaven area, and he built a Greek Revival home, marking his branch of the family as "the rich Elams."

Edward's log home was built prior to 1854, when his younger daughter, Laura, was born. That year, too, the land was transferred into the name of Elam's wife Sarah. When Sarah Elam died, the property was divided among their four daughters. In 1902, Laura Elam Sharpe purchased that portion of thirty-eight acres where the house stood from her sister, Emma

Hildebrand's heirs. The property stayed in the family till 1924.

The house is built of yellow poplar logs, twelve feet by eighteen feet square, with square corner notching, instead of crisscross design commonly associated with log cabins. This simple method of construction was typical of the era on the frontier when more sophisticated craftsmen were scarce.

The original chinking has been replaced with cement. The house is two stories with a gabled roof. Log infill below the second-story windows, and a section above the uppermost log indicate that the roof was raised to give more room in the second story.

Originally a dogtrot plan, the log section of the house has two rooms on each floor separated by a wide hall. The original rooms have plaster walls and ceilings. The living room and both second-story rooms have wooden mantels decorated with pilasters, while the downstairs bedroom has a brick fireplace with log mantel. The windows on both floors are casement.

Several additions have been made to the rear of the housing giving it a total of fourteen rooms, and a second porch has been added on the front. The earliest addition was probably made shortly after the Civil War, the others date from the 1930s to the 1960s.

The house now sits on less than one acre at an angle to its neighbors, small single family houses built in the 1950s, a quaint reminder of the frontier in the midst of modern suburbia. ∎

Buntyn-Ramsay House

1864

Geraldus Buntyn, who gave his name to the Buntyn Station neighborhood six miles east of downtown, was born in North Carolina and served as a soldier in the War of 1812. For this he received a land grant of one hundred and sixty-eight acres on the frontier in Alabama. After farming there for a few years, he moved with his wife and family to another frontier, Memphis. The new region was hospitable to him. He began buying land in the 1830s, and when he died in 1865, his estate totalled 1,405 acres, and he was rich enough to have already given each of his children $10,000. He was a respected member of the community, too, serving as a delegate from Shelby County to the Western and Southwestern Conventions of 1845, serving as a director of the Farmers and Merchants Bank and as one of the incorporators of the University of Memphis in 1846. He was a pillar of the Baptist Church, giving the land for First Baptist Church in 1845 after he had helped organize it and had led the search for a pastor in 1839. His family also gave the land for Eudora Baptist Church in 1857 and it is still located at that original site, now at Poplar and Perkins.

In the 1850s, when the Memphis and Charleston Railroad came to West Tennesse, his home was a landmark on the route just outside of Memphis and the area came to be called Buntyn's Station. He had built a large comfortable home with several verandas to house his family; the house became the first home of the Memphis Country Club before it burned in 1910. When Geraldus Buntyn died in 1865, his property was subdivided into lots of from three to ten acres. The convenience of the railroad line with its easy access to the city had made possible the development of truck and dairy farming in the area. At one point, there were so many diaries that what is now Chickasaw Gardens was known as "Buttermilk Town."

Although Geraldus Buntyn's home burned, one Buntyn family house is still standing. It was built for his son, Dr. G. O. Buntyn, in 1864, to the west of the homeplace, facing what is now Goodwyn Street.

The house looks older than its years because of the simplicity of its Federal style, which has a dignity that ornate turreted Victorian residences sometimes lack. The bricks, handmade on the property, were laid in Dutch Bond style: every seventh brick is laid crosswise, making the walls eighteen inches thick. There are hand-hewn pine floors and oak doors with the original brass hinges.

Dr. Buntyn's daughter Euzelia married George W. Rutland and they lived in the house at the turn of the century, until her death in childbirth at the age of thirty-six. In 1906 Mrs. Henry Ashton Ramsay saw a "For Rent" ad in the Sunday paper and that afternoon she took a carriage ride into the country to look at the house. She discovered that while Mr. Rutland thought it was all right to advertise on Sunday, he considered it a sin to do business and wouldn't show the house. Mrs. Ramsay had to drive back to town, but she returned another day, and the Ramsays first rented and then bought the house. Their son, Jack W. Ramsay, still lives there.

The Ramsays added a wing to the north, with brick work so perfectly matching that it is indistinguishable from the original. Originally a side hall plan, the addition makes it a center hall arrangement. There is a spacious entrance hall with a beautifully proportioned stairway. To the right (north) is the dining room with kitchen behind it. To the left (south) is the parlor; the original crystal sconces are seen in the hall and parlor. There are a total of twelve rooms.

The exterior is distinguished by mellow brick, a two-story frame portico with square pillars, a second floor balcony with turned railings and broad steps leading to the entrance. Across the south side is a two-story screened porch with railings and square pillars. Ancient crepe myrtles and tall trees surround the house. Matching gardens enclosed in white picket fences once stood on either side of the house. ∎

ABOVE:
The Buntyn-Ramsay house was built in 1864 near the railroad at Buntyn's Station.

Maxwelton 1860
(Sneed-Ewell House)

Another prominent resident of the Buntyn's Station community was Judge John Louis Taylor Sneed. He was born in North Carolina in 1820, moved as a child to LaGrange, Tennessee, became a lawyer, and moved to Memphis in 1843. In the Mexican War he was one of the Tennessee Volunteers who gave the state its nickname, and he rose to the rank of captain. In the Civil War, he was appointed a brigadier general in the Provisional Army of Tennessee by Governor Isham G. Harris.

Between the wars he held several posts: he was a member of the Tennessee General Assembly, attorney-general for Memphis in 1848, and in 1854 attorney-general of Tennessee. In 1859 he was a Whig candidate for Congress but was defeated. After the Civil War he resumed his legal career and was elected to the Tennessee Supreme Court in 1870, serving eight years. In 1879 he became a judge in the Court of Arbitration. From 1894 to 1900 he was Chancellor of Shelby County. He died in 1901.

Judge Sneed was one of the founders of St. John's Episcopal Church and a trustee of the property.

His house, called Maxwelton, at Buntyn's Station was probably built about 1860 and is still lived in by his descendent John Sneed Ewell. It is a one-story white frame house in Victorian "piano box" style. Bays at each end of the front facade are centered by a recessed

porch which gives entry into an offset central hall and has side entries to the two bays. In the western bay is a parlor with bay window and behind it a bedroom. In the eastern bay are a sitting room and bedroom, the front with a bay window matching the other side. The recessed center section contains a hall and dining room. The house sits on brick pillars with lattice between them. Above each bay window is a gable containing a ventilation grill. There are three brick chimneys. Across the rear is a series of modern rooms.

The interior has fourteen-foot ceilings and four-inch pine board floors. There are five fireplaces with wooden mantels, some with tiled hearths, and the original porcelain door knobs.

Mrs. Sneed had an extensive rose garden. The bricked flower pit measuring eight feet deep by ten feet long by four feet wide in which she used to place flowering plants for the winter is still there. The house was originally surrounded by several outbuildings, including a small frame two-room structure on the northeast corner of the property which was Judge Sneed's law office and library.

Although the 1860s are usually given as the date of the house, construction may have been earlier. Deeds and newspaper articles show the Sneed family living there by 1874, after Judge Sneed purchased the house from Levi Joy who bought the property from E. A. Spottswood in 1869. Tax records and oral history indicate the house may have been there before the 1860s.

Captain Harris House

1898

 An excellent example of frame Queen Anne style is found on Young Avenue in a house built in 1898. The builder, Frank Trimble, sold the house in 1900 to Captain Harris from Mississippi, whose move to Memphis was probably the result of a feud in which Colonel William C. Falkner, author of *The White Rose of Memphis,* was killed by a relation of Harris'. Falkner's great-grandson, William Faulkner, used the incident in two of his novels, *Requiem For a Nun* and *The Unvanquished.*

The house originally sat on a slight hill on a three-acre lot facing west. In 1925 it was turned to face Young Avenue. It is two-and-a-half stories high with a round turret under a conical roof on the southwest corner. A wide one-story veranda with bracketed posts extends across the south facade and around the turret. In the center, the veranda is interrupted by a two-story gabled entry, the second story having a pagoda-like roof. The east section has a grouping of three windows on the second floor topped by panels of sunburst carving. Above this is a semi-circular arched window in the half story. There are multiple entries on the first floor, put there when the house was converted to apartments.

The contrasting textures of clapboard and wood shingles laid in patterns, the gaily carved trim, and the irregularity of the massing make this a delightful example of Queen Anne style. ∎

ABOVE:
Contrast and variety mark the Queen Anne style Richards house, built in 1883.

AT LEFT:
*The entrance hall of the
Richards house.*

Richards House

1883

A Queen Anne house on Peabody was built by a cotton merchant in 1883. Newton Copeland Richards was born in New Orleans in 1854. When he was seventeen he went to work for a cotton company and rose through the business, being sent to Memphis in 1883 to take charge of an office there. That year was an eventful one for Richards; he married Miss Louise Mather of Louisiana and brought his bride to Memphis, where they built a house in an area called Estival Park.

Mrs. Richards died in 1892, leaving a son and a daughter. In 1902, Mr. Richards served as president of the Memphis Cotton Exchange, and he lived until 1934. It was said of him in a 1923 volume of biographies, "He has never deviated from the course which the world regards as right in the varied relations of life and measures up to the full stature of upright, honorable manhood."

The exterior of the three-story frame house is marked by typical Queen Anne-style contrast and variety. A rounded porch with turned posts and spindles leads to the entrance on the right of the facade. Above this is a balcony with circular openings and carved spindles arranged in sunburst patterns. Fish-scale shingles and grooved panelling laid both vertically and diagonally to the horizontal clapboards add to the richness of detail. The roof is the original standing-seam tin.

The entrance hall has a winding staircase and mahogany fretwork trim. A fireplace in the entrance hall was designed to send heat to the second floor at night when all the first-floor doors were closed. The parlor and dining rooms open to the left, and the dining room has floor to ceiling built-in shelves.

The ceilings are thirteen feet high; there are oak floors, mahogany woodwork and the original brass fixtures throughout. Many of the interior doors have stained glass transoms. There are tile-trimmed fireplaces throughout. The third floor is a fifteen hundred square foot attic with ten foot ceilings. ∎

AT RIGHT:
*The fortress-like
Tennessee Brewery has
been a landmark on the
bluffs since 1885.*

Tennessee Brewery

1885

OPPOSITE RIGHT:
*Millions of gallons of
beer flowed from the
many levels inside the
Tennessee Brewery.*

Twelve million barrels of beer flowed from the Tennessee Brewery in its sixty-nine years high on the bluff overlooking the river.

The brewery was founded in 1885 by John W. Schorr, who came to Memphis by way of St. Louis from Germany, where, it is said, his family had been brewers for five hundred years. Drillers for an artesian well on the bluff located a spring of pure water, just the right temperature for beer making. There Schorr built his brewery, and by 1890 he was so successful that the building had to be enlarged. By 1900 it was said to be the largest brewery in the South, employing one hundred and fifty people and continually filling twenty wagons in the courtyard. Schorr supplied dealers in Tennessee, Georgia, Alabama, Arkansas and Mississippi with his Columbian Extra Pole, Pilsner and Erlanger Brands. The success of the brewery mirrored the rising fortunes of Memphis after the yellow fever scourges of the 1870s.

John Schorr became a leader in many civic affairs, but his main love was horse racing, and his stable was famous. His horse won the Tennessee Derby at Montgomery Park (now the Fair Grounds) in Memphis in 1898 and came in second in the Kentucky Derby that year. The Tennessee Derby at the time paid more money than the Kentucky Derby, but racing was banned in Tennessee in 1906. Mr. Schorr kept trying to win the Kentucky Derby up to 1915 with horses named Ed Crump and Goldcrest Boy.

When Prohibition came, five hundred and twenty-seven people were on the payroll and Goldcrest was the brewery's most famous beer. Undaunted, Mr. Schorr closed the brewery for six weeks, then reopened, making soft drinks, as the Tennessee Beverage Company. When the ban on alcohol was lifted, the brewery was ready, too, and within a few months Mr. Schorr and his sons were producing beer at capacity again. The fifty-first anniversary of the firm was celebrated in 1936 with a new brand, Goldcrest 51, using malt from Wisconsin and hops from Czechoslovakia and Oregon.

Eventually Goldcrest became the victim of competition from nationally adverised brands. Mr. Schorr died in 1932, but his son, Jacob Schorr, and grandson, Jacob, Jr., continued to produce beer on the bluff until 1954.

The building is Richardson Romanesque in style, built around a loading court in a U-shape. The exterior is made of red brick with deeply cut stone at the base and white limestone trim. There are three distinct sections, variously four, five and six stories high. The court is entered through a tunnel under a tower that dominates the south facade. There is ornate corbelling rising above the roof line.

The interior, designed to hold heavy brewing equipment, is on different levels, connected by short cast iron staircases. Ornate cast iron columns and railings support the roof and the stairs. ∎

Marine Hospital 1 8 8 4

The Marine Hospital Service was established under President John Adams in 1798 to give aid to sick and disabled seamen; this was a predecessor of the United States Public Health Service. In 1881, Congress appropriated $30,000 for the construction of a facility in Memphis. Construction began in 1883 on a six building complex which included a surgeon's quarters, a stable, an executive building, two wards and a laundry-dining room. The original hospital was completed in 1884. In the 1930s, new buildings were constructed and the frame wards and stables were demolished; the surgeon's quarters disappeared in 1964. Thus two of the original buildings remain on the site, now surrounded by the newer parts of the complex.

The hospital has served the Coast Guard, members of the Coast and Geodetic Survey, Public Health field men, the Army Corps of Engineers, and federal workers injured on duty as well as its initial clients, seamen. In the 1950s the name was changed to the U.S. Public Service Hospital to reflect this change. Since 1965 it has ceased to be used as a health facility but houses the Army Reserve and the National Ornamental Metals Museum in some of its buildings. The tree-shaded lawn situated on a high bluff south of the river bridges commands one of the best views of the Mississippi River, near the site of former Fort Pickering.

The two original brick buildings remaining were relocated on the site in 1937. The executive building, a two-story rectangular brick building painted white, was moved about one hundred feet northwest, and a frame enclosed porch with a pedimented gable in Georgian style was added. The laundry and dining room building was also moved about one hundred feet northwest of its original location and converted to nurses' quarters, but its exterior retains its 1884 Italianate appearance. It is also a two-story rectangular brick building painted white. It has a metal hip roof with a bracketed cornice. The building is six windows long and two windows wide; the windows are set into arched openings. It is surrounded by a one-story porch with a sloped roof supported by bracketed posts and a modillioned cornice, and has a diamond patterned railing. ∎

AT RIGHT:
This 1884 brick building is one of two original buildings remaining from the Marine Hospital Service complex on the bluffs south of the Memphis-Arkansas Bridge.

SHELBY COUNTY

Seven Hills Plantation

at Woodstock

1844

Seven Hills Plantation is the oldest farm in Shelby County and has been the possession of the same family since 1821. Andrew Rembert was the descendent of French Huguenots who came to the American colonies in the 1800s seeking religious freedom. In 1819, the year that Shelby County was established, he came to West Tennessee to take up a land grant given for service in the Revolutionary War. He started building the house in north Shelby County before his death in 1845.

His son, Samuel Stokes Rembert, finished the house, and lived there with his wife, Ann Duncan, whose family owned a nearby plantation on the Loosahatchie River. The Remberts had thirteen children, only five of whom survived childhood.

The house was built of lumber cut on the place. It has a two-story central section with flanking one-story wings. A simple pediment atop four square columns is over the entrance. The house has a central hall, two square rooms on either side and one room at the back. The interior woodwork is walnut and the ceilings are twelve feet high. The house originally had a carved wooden balcony, more rooms and gingerbread ornamentation, but money was scarce after the Civil War and the extras were torn off.

Samuel Rembert lived in the house until his death in 1890. He had enrolled in the University of Virginia in the 1830s, but his family heard nothing from him until it was discovered that he had left school and was going up and down the Mississippi on a steamboat. He was a self-educated man with a love of classical literature and a creative bent. Among his many inventions were a mechanical cotton harvester and several firearms, including a ladies' pocket pistol, which he advertised as "neat, light and smaller than the cumbersome cylinder of the old revolver . . . does not deafen and ring in the ears. The universal demoralization of the times [1876] renders this necessary for every woman."

When he needed metal for his inventions, he was likely to melt down the silver spoons. One of his inventions was a bed on pulleys, attached to a clock timer. During the night, the bed rose slowly to reach the ceiling at midnight, whereupon it began its descent to reach the floor by morning.

Samuel Rembert wrote books, too. His *Philosophy of Life* was published in 1866. He wrote a book called *Soaring* which predicted that man someday would be able to soar, or fly. He collected recipes and gave advice in *Culinary Hygiene and Hygienic Cooking.* In 1876 he published *The Science of Life for the Wife at Home in Her Kitchen, Chamber and Parlor; or Hygienic Philosophy* in which he gives medical advice on the most delicate female complaints, recipes, practical hints for housework, tips on language and conversation, plus a glossary to improve his reader's vocabulary. He believed in the values of fresh air and sunshine: "Respiration, or breathing, admits of no delays; the air must be in constant supply; and so nature has it." His advice on sexual matters, while delicately stated, sounds quite modern as he "reveals nature's occult laws of life governing the number, character and sex of children and how to avoid the pains and perils of gestation and parturition."

His oldest son, Andrew, was killed at the age of eighteen at Shiloh and he sent his two younger sons, Henry and Sam, to the University of Toronto in Canada to keep them away from the fighting. He died in 1890.

His son Sam later erected a monument with a kneeling angel and the inscription:

> To my dear parents and loving sisters and my noble, gentle, brilliant and brave brother, killed for defending home against the most envious lot of cutthroats that ever cursed the face of the earth.

Rembert Williams is the fifth generation of the family to live at Seven Hills Plantation, which his great-grandfather named for the seven hills of Rome. ∎

AT LEFT:
Five generations of the Rembert family have lived at Seven Hills Plantation, built in 1844 near Woodstock.

Hints and recipes from Samuel Rembert's *The Science of Life.*

Wedding Cake. Take one pound of well-boiled wheaten grits, or rice, or corn well-boiled, a pound of flour, one cocoanut, grated, quarter pound of currants and raisins (better seeded), half a pound of powdered sugar, one pint of sweet olive oil, or sweet cream (of course everything ought to be sweet in a wedding cake), and ten eggs. Mix the grits well with the cocoanut and grits; add gradually the eggs, well beaten, and the flour, sugar and oil or cream. Kneed the whole thoroughly to a stiff dough, adding the cocoa milk if too dry and more flour if too moist, and bake in a rather quick oven — as everything should be on the "double quick" and "haste to the wedding."

Rice Bread. To a half pint rice boiled soft add a quart of flour and meal, half of each, mix with milk to make it mold like wheat bread, and ferment with yeast. A good bread for chronic diarrhea and other conditions.

Dandelion. The root is said to be an excellent substitute for coffee in flavor; the root washed (but the brown skin not scraped off as it possesses the aroma), cut up, parched, ground and boiled like coffee. It acts on the liver and bowels and also slightly narcotic and favorite medicine with a scientific physician.

Cheap Waterproof Paste. Mix oil or lard with fine pieces of India rubber, simmer over a slow fire until incorporated to the consistency of paste.

For Rheumatism, Ptyalism, Mercurial and Syphilitic Disease. Go to Hot Springs, Arkansas, where there are generally about a thousand such sufferers. It is now said that an insulated bed — the bedstead set in four glass tumblers and touching nothing else — will relieve and cure acute rheumatism. Asparagus, artichokes, alkaline drinks and soda bread are good for rheumatics - no acids.

Cayenne Pepper. Will keep the buttery and storeroom free from ants and cockroaches. If a mouse makes an entrance into any part of your dwelllings, saturate a rag with Cayenne, in solution, and stuff it into the hole, which can then be repaired with wood or mortar. No rat or mouse will eat that rag for the purpose of opening communication with a depot of supplies.

Spasms. So alarming to mothers. When expected, hot water should be kept on hand ready to give the child a warm or tepid bath all over, except the head, of course.

RALEIGH

The first white settler in the Raleigh area was a North Carolina trapper and hunter named Tapp who arrived in 1816. His only neighbors, the Chickasaw Indians, admired his ingenuity in trapping deer and bear as they went down a steep ravine for water at "Tapp's Hole."

The wooded area around the Wolf River remained virtually unsettled while Memphis grew on the fourth Chickasaw bluff; and the town of Randolph, forty-two miles up the Miississippi on the second bluff seemed its major rival. But John Overton, the proprietor of Memphis, was worried about his investment becoming "a mere harbor for a few drunken boatmen," and wanted Memphis to be at the seat of county government, lobbying in the legislature in 1822 to that end.

In 1824 a commission was appointed to fix the county seat and to Overton's dismay they chose Sanderlin's bluff, ten miles up the Wolf River. Immediately the town of Raleigh was laid out on fifty acres owned by Wilson Sanderlin and James Freeman. Five hundred and fifty dollars was appropriated for the building of a court house, and the first court sessions were held there in 1827. The town was named by Joseph Graham, first circuit clerk, in honor of his hometown, Raleigh, North Carolina.

Overton was right in thinking that the location of the courts were an impetus to growth. By 1836 Raleigh had a population of fifteen hundred people. Post coaches provided mail service as a link along plank roads to Memphis, and keel-boats carried freight to Raleigh, Rossville and LaGrange. A sawmill and a grist mill were built by Sanderlin. Taverns and hostelries opened to serve the lawyers who rode the circuit, and in 1829 an academy for boys was opened, followed eight years later by a female academy. In 1834 the small frame courthouse was replaced by a two-story brick building, and in 1842 a jail with eighteen-inch thick brick walls was built for horse thieves and slave stealers.

But the town of Memphis was growing even faster, thanks to cotton and the steamboat. In 1843 a criminal court was established within Memphis and gradually other judicial business shifted back. In 1866 the center of the county government was officially relocated. The property values at Raleigh declined and depression set in; the population dropped to three hundred. Even the stones of the courthouse were carted off to another location.

But Raleigh had one advantage over Memphis which became apparent in the epidemics of the 1870s: Raleigh's hills had freshwater springs. The citizens of Raleigh were determined to keep their air pure and in 1878 issued a quarantine against all travellers from Memphis.

The Raleigh springs had been thought of as health-giving as early as 1842. In 1866, the year the town lost its title of county seat, it gained a new identity as a health resort. Dr. Enno Sander, a chemist, analyzed three different springs and James M. Coleman, proprietor of a hotel in Raleigh, advertised:

> The compounding of so many valuable minerals in such happy combinations in these waters guarantees to the invalid that the Great Apothecary, the God of Nature, has designed them for the healing of his creatures.

But Raleigh's location was now proving a disadvantage. The Wolf River was blocked by logs and debris as population had increased along its banks. The hills were an obstacle to road builders, and railroads developed north and south but not through Raleigh. It was a dusty three-mile drive to the tracks to Memphis.

Then, in 1891, another great event occured in Raleigh's fortunes. The tobacco magnate W. Duke from Durham, North Carolina, appeared in Raleigh like a fairy godfather with $100,000 to build an electric car line to Memphis and a resort hotel. For ten years the spa was a fashionable vacation spot, a hotel with a rotunda and mezzanine, little pavillions over the springs, and orchestra music to entertain the guests. But the hotel lasted less than ten years. In 1903 it closed its doors and a fire in 1912 finally desroyed it.

Today Raleigh seems a part of Memphis instead of a distant destination. Highways, subdivisions and shopping malls have obliterated the rugged terrain. ∎

AT LEFT:
*The builder of
Goodwinslow was
inspired by medieval
castles and Italian Villas
that he saw on his
travels.*

Goodwinslow

1 8 7 5

William Washington Goodwin was a Middle Tennessean who served in General Forrest's army during the Civil War. When the war was over, he moved to Shelby County and practiced law in Memphis but every day commuted to his office from Raleigh by railroad and buggy. He had an aversion to automobiles which proved prophetic, as he was killed by a car in Court Square in 1922. Mr. Goodwin had travelled extensively in Europe and, in 1875, he began building his home on a wooded hilltop, incorporating bits of what he had seen abroad.

The house grew room by room. The north section was built in 1875, modeled after a medieval castle. The middle section was added in 1880, one story under a steeply pitched gable roof. The final sections, inspired by an Italian villa, were added in 1890 and 1900. A two-and-a-half story crenellated tower with small turrets is behind the center section.

Mr. Goodwin, was determined to build a fireproof

building as the previous house on the site had burned. Hand-baked clay bricks, stone and stucco are the materials for the walls, while the foundation is concrete and the roof is hollow clay tiles on steel beams. The diversity of form and mass, linked by stucco covering most of the exterior, make the house unique.

Various stylistic influences are seen in the twenty rooms of the interior; medieval style fireplaces co-exist with classical details such as Corinthian capitals. Mr. Goodwin's granddaughter described him as "short on cash and long on imagination." His imagination created a remarkable home for five generations of his family.

His daughter, Anne, was tutored at home and roamed the Raleigh hills. When the Raleigh Springs Hotel was built, Anne spent her summers listening to the music and watching the visitors. The Chickasaw Guards performed drills for the entertainment of the guests on weekends. One of these guests, a young captain of the U.S. Engineers, fell in love with Anne and married her. He was Eveleth Winslow, grandson of a Union admiral in the Civil War, a graduate of West Point and a Spanish-American War officer. In 1899 he was detailed to the Memphis office for work on the Mississippi River. After their marriage, they lived in Hawaii, Panama and Washington, before returning to live at Goodwinslow after her father's death.

When she was seventy, Anne Goodwin Winslow began to write, publishing six books, including novels, poetry and an autobiography. Her home became a meeting place for the artistic and literary sets, and visitors to Goodwinslow included Robert Penn Warren, Allen Tate, John Crowe Ransom, Vachel Lindsay, Ford Madox Ford, and Richard Halliburton.

The Winslows had two children: Randolph, killed in World War II, and Mary, who married Charles Chapman. Like her mother, Mary is a writer, and has published her memories of growing up in Raleigh before urban sprawl engulfed it. Her son, E. Winslow Chapman, and his son are the fourth and fifth generations to live at Goodwinslow. ∎

AT RIGHT:
An interior scene at Goodwinslow.

Graham House 1870s

ABOVE:
This house was built before the Civil War by the family of the man who gave Raleigh its name.

 When Joseph Graham, the man who named Raleigh in honor of his North Carolina birthplace, came to Tennessee, the land he acquired was located on the second highest elevation in Shelby County. Graham purchased four hundred acres from John Ralston on November 10, 1829, and the land stayed in his family until 1898. Colonel Graham died on August 18, 1837, and was buried on his land. He left three sons and one daughter. One of his descendents, Albert Graham, owned the land from 1869 to 1896, and lived in a house at the crest of a hill overlooking the Wolf River bottoms.

The house, which may have been built as early as 1856, is a one-story building of pine with two-inch-thick yellow poplar sheathing. The front porch extends the width of the house with a small triangular pediment over the entrance, and the original pillars, each made of one solid log. The house has a dogtrot plan with a chimney at each end. The floors are the original random width pine and much of the plaster work is original. ∎

BARTLETT

The town of Bartlett was incorporated in 1866 with a population of fewer than one hundred. The site was that of Union Depot, a stop along the Memphis and Ohio Railroad, where the railroad met the stage coach from Nashville.

The town was named for Major Gabriel Bartlett, who had a wholesale grocery establishment on Front Street in Memphis but lived in Bartlett along what is now the main street, which ran for half a mile westward from the railroad depot.

In 1870 Bartlett was the site of a circuit court and the courthouse at Raleigh was torn down and its bricks used for a new building in Bartlett. At first the Bartlett court had county-wide jurisdiction, but in 1873 the Memphis cases were taken from the Bartlett judge; in 1879 all the cases south of the Wolf River were transferred, and by 1885 the days of Bartlett as a courthouse town were ended.

Bartlett had two notable educational institutions: the Masonic Collegiate Institute and the Blackwell School, which had an enrollment of over one hundred pupils in 1887 when the population of the town was only three hundred.

Several old houses still stand in Bartlett, recalling the rural days of the county town, now a bustling urbanized area.

Glendale 1840s

Travellers along Interstate 40 catch a tantalizing glimpse of an old home on a rise on the north side of the highway eighteen miles from Memphis. It is Glendale, set among tall cedars and dogwoods, once the center of a thousand acre plantation.

Elijah Pulliam was born in Fredericksburg, Virginia, in 1799. He moved to Madison County, Alabama, before coming to Shelby County in 1838 and settling on a plantation near Bartlett. His house was probably built in the early 1840s, and it is said that Ace Edwards, who had supervised the design and building of Holly Hills for his brother-in-law Robert Ecklin, oversaw the building of Glendale. Like Holly Hills, Glendale is a two-story brick house with a porch across the front, simple windows with rectangular lintels, doorways on both floors with transoms and sidelights, and no windows on the east side. At Glendale, the porch extends all the way across the facade and the tall wooden columns are octagonal. A balcony used to extend the length of the porch, but it has been replaced with a smaller one.

The floor plan has a central hall with a steep stairway and square rooms opening off it on both floors. A one room ell at the rear has a small porch over an outside door. The floors, mantels and simple door moldings are original. The walls are three bricks deep, and the house has a cellar.

Elijah Pulliam married Pamela Nelson Massey in 1829, and they had thirteen children. When Pulliam died, the minister of the Bartlett Methodist Church said:

He died in great peace and triumph, on December 5, 1884, and was buried in his family burying ground, surrounded by his host of weeping relatives and friends on December 7. Brother Pulliam was the father of thirteen, eight of whom preceded him to enter the better land. His sorely bereaved wife, his companion for more than fifty-five years, and five children expect to meet him in heaven.

Charles Bryan, a Memphis lawyer and politician who gave the road on which the house is located its name, was a later resident and held political barbecues in the yard.

ABOVE:
*Glendale was built near
Bartlett in the 1840s.*

finished while they waited for the plaster to dry. But tragedy struck. His wife gave birth to one daughter, Willie, but died only two nights after they had moved into their new home. The house had six bedrooms, but it remained for the next generation to fill them. Willie married Benjamin Robinson Miller and they had four children, one of whom died in infancy, but three of whom grew up in the spacious home. Dr. Blackwell died in 1910 at the age of seventy-two, but his granddaughter Louise lived there for all of her eighty-eight years.

The house is built of white poplar in Gothic Revival Style with many gables. The rooms have twelve-foot ceilings and spacious dimensions. A semicircular porch added by Benjamin Miller curves around the front, and scroll carving ornaments the peaks of the gables. A beautifully curved mahogany staircase leads to the second floor. ∎

Blackwell House

1869

The house at the corner of Sycamore and Blackwell has known happiness and its share of tragedy — it was built by a doctor whose own wife died tragically young.

Nicholas Blackwell was born in 1838, and grew up in Pontotoc County, Mississippi. He was educated at Union University in Murfreesboro, Tennessee, and received a medical degree from Jefferson College in Philadelphia in 1860. He returned to Mississippi to go into practice with his brother George, but the Civil War intervened. Nicholas enlisted as a private in the Confederate Army and fought in the battles of Corinth, Franklin, Nashville and Atlanta, rising to the rank of captain. After the war he moved to Bartlett at the urging of his uncle, John Blackwell, one of the leading citizens of the area.

Nicholas joined his uncle as one of the most prominent men in their neighborhood, and he donated the land upon which the courthouse was built. When the court closed, he loaned the building for a school. He was a much-loved physician, riding into the country at night to tend the sick with hot bricks at his feet to keep him warm.

He married Miss Virginia Ward, and they began to build their home. They boarded nearby while the house was being built, and stayed on after it was

Smith-McKenzie House

1850s

The oldest house still standing in Bartlett was built about 1850, before the town was incorporated, for a Mr. and Mrs. Smith who were reported to have been school teachers in Memphis and to have used the Bartlett house as a summer home. It is in this house that Dr. Nicholas Blackwell and his wife rented rooms while their house was being built next door.

The house originally sat on a large tract of land surrounded by outbuildings; remnants of the original kitchen have been found under the garden. It is a two-story white frame house with a simple Greek Revival pediment supported by posts of an unusual open lattice-work design. Lattice-work pilasters are on either side of the entrance, which has sidelights and a square transom topped by dentil molding. Two dormer windows on the second floor have a Greek Key design in the molding. The house sits on a raised open-work brick foundation.

An unusual feature is the Egyptian Revival door moldings on the interior, which imitate the shape of Egyptian temple entrances, the molding being broader at the bottom with a gentle slope toward the square-cornered lintel at the top. ■

AT LEFT ABOVE:
The interior doors of the Smith-McKenzie house imitate the form of Egyptian temple entrances.

AT LEFT BELOW:
Lattice-work pillars support the pediment of the Smith-McKenzie house in Bartlett.

Yates-Marr House

1870s

A Victorian "piano box" style house sits under tall trees on Sycamore View Road in Bartlett. The exterior is white clapboard and the recessed front porch has a turned railing and six pillars. The spacious one-story home has four bedrooms, parlor, dining room, kitchen, and porches. Nearly every room has a small fireplace with coal grate and the ceilings throughout are fourteen feet high.

The house was built in the 1870s by Tom Yates, a veteran who lost one arm in the Civil War. He and his wife raised three children there, Foster, Tate and Mattie. In 1922 the Yates heirs sold the property to Helen M. Lilly (of the Lilly Carriage Company family) for "Ten dollars cash in hand and other good and valuable considerations." Later the house was occupied by Clarence Saunders of Piggly Wiggly fame. ∎

BELOW:
The Yates-Marr house in Bartlett is a Victorian "piano box" style.

Nicholas Gotten House 1884

 The house now owned by the Bartlett Historical Society was for a time the Bartlett Police Station. But for sixty-four years it was the home of the Gotten family.

Nicholas Gotten was born in Prussia in 1832, coming to seek his fortune in the United States at the age of twenty-two, and making his way South to settle in the Bartlett area in 1860, where he set up as the town blacksmith. When the Civil War broke out he was eager to enlist in the cause of his adopted area, but friends convinced him that he was needed at home where he could aid the community and help provide arms for the troops. But after the fall of Ft. Donelson, "his blood boiled with the heat of war," according to *Confederate Military History*, and he enlisted as a private in Forrest's regiment. After fighting at Shiloh, Corinth and other engagements, he was wounded at Bolivar in 1864. He tried to rejoin his regiment but was taken prisoner and sent to the infamous Irving Block on Court Square in Memphis. Finally he was able to

rejoin the army until its surrender. During his service he did double duty as a soldier and as a blacksmith.

After the war he returned to Bartlett, and married Julia Coleman in 1869. The next year he bought land and may have lived in a small house on the property until his larger house was built in 1884. They had three children: Peter Monroe, David Henry and Maggie Amelia. Nicholas Gotten's land was divided between them with Maggie inheriting the house, but she moved to Chicago and sold the house to David's widow, Leona, for ten dollars. It remained in the family until 1948.

The house is white frame with three gables on the facade. A simple porch covers the center, with a balcony above the entrance. It is built in the New England salt-box style with one-and-a-half stories and a sloping roof at the back. There are seven rooms, five on the first floor and two in the half story. The entrance door has a square transom and sidelights. Its lack of decoration gives it an austerity unusual in the area.

■

ABOVE:
Nicholas Gotten's house, built in 1884 in Bartlett, is an unusual salt-box shape.

Davies Manor at Brunswick

1807

Davies Manor is considered the oldest house in Shelby County. Tradition says that the west portion of the two-story log house was built about 1807, possibly by an Indian. The recorded history of the house begins with Joel W. Royster, who built the eastern portion and connecting dog trot after he acquired the property in 1831.

In 1851 Royster sold the log house and surrounding land to Logan Early Davies. Davies and his brother James Baxter Davies were the sons of William E. Davies, a Methodist minister from Maury County, Tennessee, and grandsons of Zachariah Davies, a Revolutionary War militiaman from Lunenburg County, Virginia. The brothers acquired land around Brunswick which eventually totalled two thousand acres, and is still owned by their descendant, Mrs. Ellen Davies Rodgers. Mrs. Rodgers gave the house to the Davies Manor Association in 1976, and it is open to the public as a museum and is available for the use of patriotic societies.

The road at the entrance to Davies Plantation (now Highway 64) was the stagecoach route from Memphis to Nashville through Raleigh, Morning Sun, and Sommerville. During the Civil War both armies used this road. In 1863 Union soldiers came through the plantation and rounded up all the livestock. Frances Anna Vaughn Davies, the wife of Logan E. Davies, saw that the officer in charge had her own horse. She got a kitchen knife and hid it in the folds of her skirt. Speaking to the officer as she would to a gentleman, she asked him twice to leave her horse. When he refused, she took the horse by the bridle and cut the reins with her knife. "Sir," she said, "I have my horse. You go." He went.

The house sits on its original foundation of sandstone pillars in a thirty acre grove of trees with an Indian mound on the east side. It is built of squared hand-hewn white oak logs with square-notched corners. The earliest section was a twenty-foot-square room with a second room above it. An identical section was added by Royster probably about the time of the Mexican War, at least before 1850. The dogtrot connecting the two wings was enclosed in 1931 and earlier additions to the back were improved in 1942.

ABOVE/RIGHT:
The western portion of Davies Manor is considered the oldest remaining house in Shelby County, built about 1807.

Griffin House at Brunswick

1 8 6 0 s

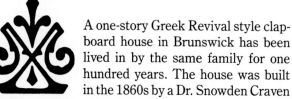

A one-story Greek Revival style clapboard house in Brunswick has been lived in by the same family for one hundred years. The house was built in the 1860s by a Dr. Snowden Craven Maddux, who sold it in 1882 to the John Griffins, whose son's widow lives there now.

The house was a typical four room central hall plan when it was built. The kitchen and dining room were in the basement. The Griffins added rooms across the back in the 1880s. It retains many of the original doors and much wainscoting in the interior. It has a simple porch with four square pillars and tall windows on each side. The door has an arched transom and fluted pilasters. ∎

AT RIGHT:
*The Griffin house,
Brunswick.*

Cedar Hall at Ellendale   1 8 4 0 s

Like many towns in Shelby County in which the early history of the community is primarily the story of one family, Ellendale was called Bond's Station for its early settlers, the Bonds. In 1831 Margaret Ann Bond, a widow, and her three sons moved to Shelby County. Her husband, Nicholas Pirtle Bond, had served under General Andrew Jackson in the Creek Indian war. The family had moved from Knox County, Tennessee, to Limestone County, Alabama, where Nicholas Bond died in 1831, leaving his heirs title to land in Tennessee.

Peggy Bond and her sons came to clear the wilderness. Two of her sons, Washington and Samuel, were doctors, and the third, John, a planter. They first lived in a dirt-floored log cabin, but soon prospered. Mrs. Bond's tombstone in Ellendale Cemetary gives her life span as 1781 to 1862.

John Bond built a big log house which served as a stage stop and post office for the Green Bottom community. He joined the Green Bottom Cumberland Presbyterian Church in 1833 and gave the land for the church (which later joined with the Morning Sun congregation) and for the school. His descendents continued to farm his land, fronting on today's Highway 64.

Dr. Sam Bond had been educated at Cumberland College in Lebanon, Tennessee, and at the medical school of Transylvania University in Lexington, Kentucky, while his family still lived in Alabama. A letter written in 1825 while Sam was still at school tells of his visiting General Jackson and inspecting the general's collection of firearms. In 1829 he married Mary Lucy Tate, daughter of Jesse Tate, whose family had also moved to Shelby County, and who had lived in the Wyatt house on Beale Street.

Dr. Sam and his bride moved westward with his mother and brothers. About 1840 he built a house which later burned. In 1844 he gave up his medical practice for his first love, farming. In 1847 he served one term in the Tennessee General Assembly; while there, he introduced a bill to incorporate the Memphis and Holly Springs Railroad, gaining railroad stock and his name on one of the stations.

ABOVE:
Cedar Hall at Ellendale
was built in the 1840s by
Dr. Samuel Bond.

After his first house burned, he built, in the late 1840s, a three-story brick house which still stands. He called it "The Avenue" for the row of cedars leading to the entrance. Today the house is known as Cedar Hall. It is Greek Revival style with an impressive portico with dentil molding supported by two unusual round brick columns with square capitals. Two pilasters with fluted scroll capitals are on either side of the doorway which has sidelights and an arched transom. There is a standing seam metal roof with a cornice ornamented by dentil molding. The windows have a Greek Key design on the lintels. A door leads to a balcony on the second floor above the entrance.

After his first wife died, Dr. Sam married again in Louisiana. He had many children, but few survived him. He mortgaged his Shelby County holdings which in 1855 measured seven hundred and twelve acres, to support a plantation in Carroll County, Louisiana, which he hoped would advance his agricultural fortunes. But by the time of the Civil War he saw his property swept away. Broken in health and fortune, he died in 1862 at the age of fifty-seven.

In 1870 the Shelby County property passed to an Englishman, Edmund Orgill (1825-1905), the first of his name in Tennessee. Orgill had come to Memphis and, in 1847, founded a firm handling hardware, nails, agricultural implements and tools. His descendents carry on that firm today. The Orgills lived at "The Avenue" for about thirty-five years with one interesting exception. For three years in the 1880s the home was leased to another Englishman, Lord Thomas Marsh Horsfall, who held elaborate Masonic events there. On July 16, 1883, the Knights Templar Masonic Lodge filled a special car on the railroad from Memphis to Bond's Station with guests in full Masonic regalia.

As with many communities, the railroad was the agent of change. Dr. Sam Bond had brought the first line there and given the station his name. The Memphis and Ohio Railroad took over in 1855, extending from the riverfront in Memphis through Union Station (Bartlett), then Bond's Station, Brunswick, Pea Point, and Wythe Depot (Arlington). Despite its name the M & O had only gotten as far as Paris, Tennessee, by the time the Civil War broke out.

The Louisville and Nashville Railroad took over the line after the war. About 1909, the L & N held a contest to rename Bond's Station. A Mrs. Justice won by suggesting Ellendale (L & N and dale). The town was incorporated by the state legislature in 1909, and the Ellendale Land Company soon published a pamphlet advertising "convenient suburban homes" in an area to be developed as 150 five-acre "community farms." With extravagant claims about the profits to be made ("It is not too much to expect $1,000 worth of flowers from one acre in a season"), the developers boasted of beauty and convenience:

> The men behind Ellendale are citizens of the highest business character and are well known in Memphis and Shelby County and may be depended upon to carry out any statements they may make. With the wonderful strides now being made in intensive farming, your independence lies in your power of production, and Community Farms now offer you the means of reaching your goal and living in an environment that you will be proud of.

CORDOVA

Morning Sun, Green Bottom, Sanga, Bethany and Dexter — all of these names speak of rural settlements now encompassed in the community of Cordova.

The first settlers were North Carolinians — two brothers, Robert and Joshua Ecklin, their two sisters and their husbands, Sabrina and William Patrick, and Betsy and Thomas Allen — who came in the fall of 1835, and began to farm near what is now Macon Road. They and their descendents carved farmland from the wilderness. Cotton was the cash crop, ginned with a gin they had brought with them from North Carolina.

By 1838 other families — Greens, Coles, Rogers and Galloways — had settled to the south and west along what is now Germantown Road and Raleigh-La-Grange Road.

The first name of the settlement was Marysville, in honor of Miss Mary Williams, but the name was changed to Allentown about 1875 because of the many Allen families. Mr. Jim Allen, whose store was on the south side of Macon Road, gave the land for the Presbyterian Church, the cemetery, the school and two lots for the Baptist preacher and the Presbyterian minister and teacher, Professor Allen. When the first railroad, the Tennessee Midland, came through in 1888, the town was named Dexter, and finally became Cordova in 1903, as the railroad wanted to avoid duplication in the names of stops. ∎

Ecklin House 1840s

Robert Ecklin and his brother Joshua came to Shelby County in the fall of 1833 looking for opportunities to purchase good farm land. They found what they were seeking and returned to North Carolina to recruit their relatives and friends for the western trip. In January, 1835, a caravan of thirty wagons, carrying wives, children, slaves, household goods, tools, seeds, and seedlings started out, arriving in the Cordova area just in time for spring planting.

In the caravan were the two Ecklin brothers, two of their sisters and their families. In 1837 more relatives and friends joined them in clearing the wilderness for farm land. Robert Ecklin built a cypress log cabin on the Hall Road and bought additional tracts of land.

ABOVE:
The Ecklin house near Cordova was built in the 1840s, possibly by the same builder who designed Glendale.

Around 1840 he married Lucinda Edwards and enlisted the aid of her brother, Ace, in designing and building a fine brick home just a short distance from his log house. At the time, the house was the finest home outside of Memphis.

It has a central hall plan with long windows on either side of the entrance. There is a two-story porch with square columns. The entrance has side and transom lights, and above it, on the second floor, a door gives on to a small balcony. The mellow pink brick was fired on the place. Originally there were no windows on the east side and the house was surrounded by log outbuildings, a kitchen and slave quarters.

The Ecklins were a well-to-do county family and the house was the center of much social life. Descendents remember big brass keys hanging by the dining room door; they opened the smokehouse and closets containing whiskey and food. The children particularly loved the Christmas celebration, when the double doors to the front parlor would be thrown open to reveal a gay candlelit Christmas tree.

There were six children who married into the neighboring Feild and Crenshaw families. Each of the four daughters had her own personal maid, and all of the daughters went to finishing schools.

Grandmother Lucinda Ecklin is remembered by the family as sitting close beside the fire ("so the children couldn't step on her corns"), a shawl round her shoulders, a Bible open on her lap, a clay pipe in her mouth and red hair sticking out from under her cap.

After several owners, the house again rings to the sounds of gaiety as part of Holly Hills Country Club. ∎

Mt. Airy

1 8 3 5 - 5 8

 Mt. Airy is a two-story plantation home in the Morning Sun community, built about 1835 by Thomas C. Crenshaw, husband of Ellen Feild. For six generations it has been the home of the Feild family. The house is of solid log construction with yellow poplar siding put on with hand-made square nails. Inside, the walls are plastered over hand split lathes, the floors are wide white ash boards, one inch thick. The rooms are all twenty feet by twenty feet and each has a large fireplace.

The original house has a wide hall with one room on either side and three rooms upstairs. The outside doors have transoms and sidelights; the windows are nine panes with small side windows. Originally this part of the house had a double porch with columns, and today there is a small one story porch.

The Feild and Crenshaw families came to Tennessee from Petersburg, Virginia. Charles Granison Feild was the guardian for the two young children of his brother who had died, Ellen and Roscoe. Ellen married Thomas Crenshaw, who had been tutor to her brother. Their Uncle Charles returned to Virginia leaving Crenshaw in charge of Roscoe's affairs until he came of age.

Roscoe Feild graduated from Princeton in 1848, but instead of coming home to Tennessee, joined the Forty-niners in the California gold rush. By 1855 he

had returned home, and Mt. Airy plantation, with over two thousand acres, was deeded to him. In 1858 he added a two-story south wing with two rooms upstairs, a kitchen and dining room downstairs and long porches on both floors.

In 1861 he married Emily Augusta Ecklin, whose family had come from North Carolina. Her wedding band was made of California gold. He served as a captain under General Albert Sydney Johnson in the Confederate Army and was wounded at Dalton, Georgia, and sent home. Throughout the war he carried a Greek Bible, saying it was impossible to keep an English one.

Mt. Airy was in the path of both armies during the war. The wheat fields were burned and the stock driven off. Emily's father, Robert Ecklin, saw the flames and rode through the burning fields with his horse covered with wet blankets to see about his daughter and her young son.

Mt. Airy was a self-contained working plantation with its own gin, sawmill, barns, blacksmith shop and smokehouse. Cattle, sheep and cotton sustained the plantation. In 1976 it was awarded a Century Farm Certificate for being continuously operated by one family for over one hundred years. It is still a working farm with cattle, wheat, hay and soy beans the main crops.

ABOVE:
Mt. Airy near Cordova has been home to generations of the Crenshaw and Field families.

ARLINGTON

AT RIGHT:
*Tall Cedar Cottage,
1872.*

FAR RIGHT:
Will-Hugh, 1890.

In the northeastern part of Tennessee's most urbanized county, not far from the Tipton and Fayette county lines, lies Arlington, a reminder of rural village life. Pioneering farmers had settled in the area in the 1830s, but it was not until the coming of the railroad in 1856 that the village took shape as Wythe Depot. About five acres of land were donated by General Samuel Jackson Hays, a nephew of Andrew Jackson, to be used for the depot and other public uses. The community had a population of about two hundred, with two boarding houses, two general stores, a cotton gin and a gristmill. The first store in the town was built by John Dwyer. His stock consisted mainly of bad whiskey, for it is said the whiskey came near to drowning out the fire when the building burned. In 1866 the Wythe Depot post office was established. The same year General Hays died, and his will stated that a town was to be laid off around Wythe Depot; his son Robert Butler Hays moved to the area and named streets for his friends and relatives.

The name was changed to Haysville, and on May 25, 1872, a public auction of lots was held. The advertisement stated:

> Its healthy location. . . finest agricultural region. . . churches, schools. . . railroads make Haysville one of the most desirable points for business and residences. . . The people of the surrounding country are invited to be present and partake of a sumptuous barbecue which will be provided for the occasion.

The town was legally incorporated as Haysville in 1878. The same year saw the terrible yellow fever epidemic in Memphis, and the new town's mayor and aldermen enacted an ordinance strictly quarantining persons from other towns and cities from entering.

When the town was incorporated it was discovered that there was another Haysville post office, so a new

name had to be found. The name Arlington was suggested by Captain Henry Munger Pitman, builder of the first house in town, who had visited the nation's capital and had been impressed by the national cemetery. The name was changed in 1883 and a second incorporation of the town as Arlington took place in December, 1900, by which time the town boasted six hundred inhabitants and eighteen businesses.

Much of the life of the town revolved around S. Y. Wilson's General Store, which was established in 1893, selling dry goods, groceries, feed, seed, hardware and coffins, even providing hearses for hire. The pot-bellied stove was the gathering place for the men and boys of the town where gossip, tall tales and jokes were exchanged. Tobacco juice, mud and dirt were plentiful. The stove was surrounded by a wide space for sand in case of fire or sparks, and the sand also served as a spittoon.

Mr. Sam Wilson, mayor of Arlington, still operates the store founded by his grandfather, in the location it has occupied since 1912. The merchandise has changed with customers' needs and now features agricultural chemicals along with the hardware. Mr. Wilson tells a story about the old store and his fastidious aunt. The lady wore false teeth, but was so secretive about them that even her husband had never seen her without them. One day while she was in the store, she sneezed, and her teeth flew out and landed in the sand around the stove. Without flinching, she had them back in her mouth in seconds, sand and all.

While many towns in Shelby County have lost their historical character through new construction, Arlington has retained its turn-of-the-century charm, and many structures dating from 1880 to 1920 demonstrate rural vernacular architecture. Among these are:

Green Gables, built in 1887 by Samuel Jackson Beane on Walker Street, is a one-story frame house with two gables on the facade. There is pierced woodwork in the peak of each gable, with fish scale shingles and a sunburst panel. Each gable has a tall narrow window with inside shutters, topped by a pointed bonnet supported by brackets. In the center of the facade is a porch with a pointed roof and a variety of carved decoration, supported by posts with sunburst brackets.

Will-Hugh on Chester Street is a two-story frame

AT LEFT:
The Marley house,
1870.

BELOW:
The Shelton house,
1880.

ABOVE:
Green Gables, 1887.

house with a projecting gabled bay on the north of the facade. A round two-story bay is on the northern side. A one-story porch extends across the front from the gable. The house was built in 1890 by Crittenden Williams and lived in by four generations of the Williams and Hughes family. Mrs. Mabel Williams Hughes was president of the national PTA, county school superintendent and first woman state senator. Her husband and son also served in the state legislature.

The Marley House on Brown Street was built about 1870 by the second mayor of Arlington. A frame house, it has a gable with carved bargeboards and a porch across the rest of the front. A bay window in the gable has a decorated cornice.

Tall Cedar Cottage was built on Campbell Street by J.A. Mercer in 1872. It has a U-shaped plan with four chimneys. A porch on the east side extends over a handsome carved door with glass in the upper half.

The Herron House was built in 1889 and moved by wagon to its present location on Campbell Street in 1912. It is a two-story house with a curving one-story porch. The facade has three gables with fish scale shingles under the eaves.

The Shelton House on Chester Street was built about 1880 by Edward W. Shelton. It is a one-story structure with a rounded porch topped with spindle molding above bracketed posts.

Dr. G. P. Bone, a Kentuckian who was the town's first physician, built a two-story frame house on Hickory Withe in 1878. There is scrolled carving under the eaves of one large and two small gables, and a projecting bay window trimmed with rope carving and acorn finials. The house is bolted together, rather than nailed, for strength. Its construction was slowed by the outbreak of yellow fever, when two of the workmen died.

AT LEFT:
The Bone house, 1878.

BELOW:
The Herron house,
1889.

GERMANTOWN

Today's Germantown, with its handsome houses and crowded shopping centers, is a far cry from the quiet village that had one hundred and ninety-seven people in 1870 and only two hundred and sixty-three people in 1920. But traffic has followed the main artery through Germantown for many years. Busy six-lane Poplar Avenue follows the route of one of the three main Indian trails connecting the Fourth Chickasaw Bluff and the Chickasaw towns at Pontotoc, Mississippi. For centuries animals had used the ridge to avoid flooding in the lowlands, and Indians who lived as far away as three hundred miles followed the trail to trade on the Bluff.

North of Germantown's center is the Wolf River, called Nashoba by the Indians who navigated it from their cities in northern Mississippi to the Mississippi River. After LaSalle's visit to the Bluff in 1682, the river appeared on French maps as "Margot," or "Blackbird." In their struggles with the Chickasaws during the next century, the French tried to use the river as access to the Chickasaw towns but found it difficult to navigate in their long boats and finally gave up their attempts.

English and American traders found the Chickasaws more welcoming. Settlers began to come into western Tennessee after the Chickasaw Cession of 1819. Two wealthy Scots sisters were among the first visitors to the village at Memphis. Frances and Camilla Wright were protegees of LaFayette, and through him had been introduced to Thomas Jefferson and thence to Andrew Jackson. They had visited the United States in 1818, and Fanny Wright had been much moved by the general acceptance of slavery, which she saw as the flaw in the new nation's promise. By 1825 she put forth her solution: she would buy a number of slaves and set up a colony where they would

be trained to be self-supporting, and thus prepared for freedom, which they would earn as part of a producing farm community. At Jackson's invitation, she came to Tennessee to find a site for her colony. She bought the first three hundred acres of what was to become a two thousand acre estate on the Wolf River for nine cents an acre, and called it Nashoba, the Indian word for wolf. Here she established a co-operative community "in perpetual trust for the benefit of the Negro Race."

Fanny, Camilla, a few disciples and a small number of slaves set out to clear the land and build cabins. The reality was far from the utopia of her dreams. There was little time to teach the slaves to read and write, much less the philosophy of freedom. Sick and running out of money, Fanny spent months away from Nashoba, trying to gain the support of philanthropists in Europe and the north. During her absences little progress was made; instead, Nashoba earned the hostility of its neighbors with rumors of sexual promiscuity. By 1828 the experiment was doomed. Thirty-one black residents were left, but their future was unclear. In January, 1830, Frances Wright and the entire black population of Nashoba sailed from New Orleans to Haiti, where she gave them their freedom.

Frances Wright was ahead of her time in recognizing slavery as the flaw in America's character. Despite its failure, Nashoba was called by historian John Egerton "one of the first and one of the few experimental attempts to find an alternative to slavery." Frances Wright lived for another twenty-two years, crusading for other social reforms, but died a largely forgotten figure. Nashoba was left to her daughter, Sylva D'Arusmont Guthrie, but there were legal entanglements which were only settled in 1878. Today Nashoba exists only in a street name, history books and the legend of a few forlorn ghosts in the mists of a sulphur spring.

While Fanny Wright's experiment was struggling along on the banks of the Wolf, other settlers were coming into Shelby County, attracted by the promise of rich land. The ridge that had served as an Indian trail was an obvious choice for a settlement as the bottom lands were impassable during rainy weather. In 1832 a blacksmith named Thomas L. Moody cleared a plot of land off today's Germantown Road and became the town's first resident. The hamlet was called Pea Ridge. Others were quick to follow. As early as 1834, Colonel G.P. Shepherd laid off a subdivision of his land.

The Methodists held prayer meetings from the beginning of the settlement. In 1838, the Germantown Presbyterian Church was organized with eight members; by 1851 the congregation was able to build its present building. Also in 1838, the New Hope Baptist Church reported a revival which brought in forty-nine members. In 1841 Wilks Brooks donated a plot of land and the name was changed to the Germantown Baptist Church.

The town was incorporated on December 28, 1841. The building of a plank road in 1849 and the coming of the Memphis and Charleston Railroad in 1852 boosted the economy. A railroad guidebook in 1852 spoke of Germantown's two hotels, two churches, a cotton gin, a factory, a boys' school, a girls' school, and the Shelby Classical and Military Institute. There were three resorts in evergreen groves: Nashoba, White Sulphur and Brunswick Springs. The guidebook went on to say, "The inhabitants are generally moral, intelligent, and a reading people."

Why the name Germantown? There are at least three theories: for the number of German families in the area, for a man name German who surveyed the railroad, or in honor of Anthony Lucken, a German-born innkeeper. In the heat of patriotism aroused by World War I, there was an attempt to change the name to Nashoba, but after the war the name reverted to Germantown.

The Civil War did much more damage to Germantown than to the city of Memphis. Union troops were camped to the north and east and the newspapers of the time published reports of damage done by stragglers from the Federal army who wantonly broke into almost every house and store and pillaged at random.

The destruction of the businesses and the surrounding farms sent the village into a decline; in 1870 the population was one hundred and ninety-seven inhabitants. Although some citizens of Memphis bought lots during the 1870s, hoping to escape the yellow fever epidemics, Germantown was not spared, and in 1878 reported forty-five deaths from the plague. In 1900 the population was one hundred and eighty. The great population boom in Germantown was left to the second half of the twentieth century. ∎

Germantown Presbyterian Church 1851

 The eight original members of the Germantown Presbyterian congregation first met together on March 24, 1838, with the Reverend A.G. McNutt, who served as pastor until 1844. In 1850 Richard R. Evans became pastor; he served the church for fifty-three years, until his death in 1903 at the age of eighty-five. Worship services for white and black members were held in the union school house and in the Baptist Church until 1851. By November 2 of that year the Presbyterian Church building was sufficiently completed to house the congregation for the first time.

The church members passed resolutions expressing their thanks to their Baptist brethren ". . . for the privilege of worshipping God in their sanctuary for so many years." The resolutions also included an offer to return the favor should the Baptists ever require it. Little did the members of both congregations realize how soon the need would arise: the Baptist sanctuary was destroyed during the Civil War. The Presbyterian Church would have met a similar fate had not the Reverend Evans been successful in persuading the Federal commander to spare it.

Work continued on the building after the initial worship service in 1851; chimneys were erected by Mr. Jefferys and stoves were installed by March 10, 1852. The Sabbath School was organized on March 21 by Mr. Evans, and on November 10 the building committee appointed Mr. Moses Neely to arrange for plastering the interior. The plastering was finished by November 29, and the handmade pews built by Mr. Thurman Edmondson were installed and are still in use. The church was dedicated on May 14 and 15, 1853. Although it escaped destruction during the Civil War, some damage was incurred as the Union Army used the building as a hospital and stable.

The 1851 sanctuary is built in the style of the colonial meetinghouses of the preceding century: a rectangular white frame building with five green-shuttered windows on each side. The severe facade is relieved by a flight of steps leading directly to a large entry door beneath a transom. In the gable above the door is a twelve-pointed flower ventilation grill. An octagonal bell tower with paired corbels supporting the cornice and rounded dome was added in 1867.

In 1950 the building was turned on its original site facing north to face east, and placed above a raised basement instead of piers. A small portico was added, and additions were made at the rear. ∎

Germantown Baptist Church

1 8 7 0

 New Hope Baptist Church, organized in 1835, and Pea Ridge Baptist Church, organized in 1833, are the ancestors of the Germantown Baptist Church. By 1838 they had combined to form the Germantown congregation. In the early years they shared meeting space with the Presbyterians and the Methodists. As the Baptist Church grew in Germantown, two men were particularly important: Lemuel Hall Bethel, the pastor who conducted a re- vival that united forty-nine souls with the church, and Wilks Brooks, who donated the land on which the present building stands in 1841. The next year the church had a membership of seventy whites and fourteen blacks.

The building that was erected in the 1840s was burned board by board for warmth during a snowstorm by Union Troops during the Civil War; only the Bible from the pulpit was saved. The church was at a low ebb after the war and membership dropped to forty. The congregation sued the United States Government for the damages to the church, finally receiving a settlement. By 1870 the congregation was strong enough to erect another building which served them for one hundred years. In the 1970s a large new sanctuary was built to the north, and the quaint white building is used as a chapel today.

It is a rectangular frame building with five tall windows on each side. There are paired scrolled brackets under the cornice and pilasters accentuating the corners. A small triangular pediment surmounts the tall double doors at the entrance; a transom with two panes is under the pediment. The square tower with pointed steeple is visible for a distance.

Although the exterior looks the same, the interior seating was different in 1870: women entered by one side and sat together while men entered by another. ∎

Shepherd-Arthur House

1 8 4 9

The exterior of the Shepherd-Arthur House on Old Poplar Pike retains its ante-bellum appearance. The house was built in 1849 by one of the Shepherd family, who were large landowners in the early days of Germantown. It remained in that family until 1936.

The house is a frame cottage with center hall plan, twelve foot ceilings, and one square room on each side of the hall, The woodwork, fireplaces and doors are original. There are two tall windows on either side of the entrance, with dark shutters. A small porch with octagonal pillars centers the facade. The doorway has double windows in the transom. ■

BELOW:
The Shepherd-Arthur house, Germantown.

Williams House

1 8 6 0 s

Said to be one of the oldest houses in Germantown, the Williams house has had many owners. Most of the owners lived there for only short periods of time before the present owners, who bought the house in 1955, and so have been the longest residents.

The land was part of a large tract owned by Mrs. Nicey B. Shepherd of Marshall County, Mississippi, who sold sixty-three acres to Robert M. Galloway in 1850. Galloway subdivided the land, and in 1851 G.W. Frick and James Beurer bought a lot, which they sold in 1854 to S.C. Toof for three hundred dollars. Toof's wife sold a piece on the west to John M. Gray in 1856 and the main lot to Louisa Furstenheim in 1861. The

house was probably built by the time the Furstenheims sold to Mary B. Rhodes in 1870. There were more owners, including D. T. Porter, Trustee, and the Shelby County Building and Loan Association, before the postmaster of Germantown, Mr. Anderson, bought it in 1889.

The house is unusual in that it is the only early house in the neighborhood with a basement and a full second story. It originally had a two-story porch across the front and on the east side. The original house consists of two twenty-foot-square rooms on each floor on either side of a central hall, and a one-story ell at the rear. Ceilings are twelve feet on the first floor and ten on the second. There are interior chimneys at each end.   ∎

Whitlow House

1 8 7 0 s

A typical Victorian cottage sits behind a rail fence on Old Poplar Pike. It has a porch with spindle molding, scrolled bargeboards and a diversity of exterior siding. The projecting bay at the side has paired windows surrounded by horizontal clapboard and fish scale shingles with small curved brackets under the roof.

The property was part of Charles McClung's original eight hundred acre grant. On June 21, 1838, Dr. J. M. M. Cornelius purchased one hundred and eight acres of that grant from F. Siedakum by his attorney, James Titus. Cornelius held the property for nearly fifty years, selling a smaller portion to Mrs. Florida C. Thompson for two hundred and eighty dollars in 1884. Whether the Cornelius family or the Thompson family built the house is unknown, but it was on the property before the turn of the century, and has been lovingly restored. ∎

BELOW:
*The Sullivan house in
Germantown is an
example of the Carpenter
Gothic style.*

Sullivan House

1 8 6 0 s

A charming Gothic cottage nestled in azaleas has been a Germantown landmark since the Civil War. The peaked center gable with scrolled bargeboards, the pointed window and scrolled brackets in the eaves typify the Carpenter Gothic style. The house is built of poplar with square nails. There is a center hall with two rooms on each side and the ceilings are twelve feet high.

At one time boys from the nearby military school boarded in the house. A widow, Mrs. Booth, sold it in 1895 to Mr. Turner. In 1898 Minor Callis bought it, then sold it to his brother A. T. Callis, in 1900. The present owner, daughter of A. T. Callis, says that her mother, who was born in 1862, remembered walking past the house in her childhood and noticing the lovely crepe myrtles. ∎

Woodlawn

1835

"Wilks Brooks and son, Joseph, arrived at Memphis from North Carolina on 15th October, 1834, and my family (wife Patsy and children) arrived from North Carolina on the 4th December, 1835, and moved to the plantation the 20th February, 1836." So states the Brooks family Bible, thus documenting the completion date of Woodlawn, the earliest example of Greek Revival architecture in the Memphis area.

Wilks Brooks rode his horse over the mountains of Tennessee and North Carolina to look over and establish his purchase of a grant of six hundred and forty acres from Tignol Jones, a part of the original 1822 John Rice grant. Brooks made more investments in land, buying properties from Eppy White, Thomas Cole, Sugar McLemore, T. C. Nelson, T. Rutherford, T. Henderson, Frazer Titus, T. Haraleson, Thomas Cogbill, E. W. Plunkett, William Hewlett, and J. W. Callis. He had probably known many of these men in North Carolina, where he had served as a member of the General Assembly and as a delegate to the State Constitutional Convention in 1823.

The area where Wilks Brooks established his plantation was first called Pea Ridge, then Massey, and finally Ridgeway, Tennessee. Brooks built his home and surrounded it with log cabins, cisterns, a cotton gin, a blacksmith shop, a barn, chicken house, smokehouse and saw mill. His son Joseph built a country store and house nearby. When the Memphis and Charleston Railroad came in the 1850s, a hexagon-shaped brick station with two small grates for heat was built. The road, Old Poplar Pike, was dusty in hot weather and a muddy trail in rainy weather and finally became a plank road moved northward next to the railroad.

During the Civil War, Union troops camped in the woods around the house, and on one occasion tried to set the house on fire. A soldier rode by and threw hot coals on the porch, but the fire was extinguished. Later the fact that the house was used as a hospital probably saved it from destruction. Family tradition says that Mrs. Brooks was often asked to play the piano for the wounded soldiers. The Federal troops took whatever they needed in the way of chickens, cows, mules, horses, hay, lumber, corn, and wagons. When Agnes Nelson Dandridge Brooks, widow of Joseph Brooks, filed a claim for the damages later, the Congress de-

nied her claim, as "her husband was a man of means."

The Brooks house is an ell-shaped two-story frame house with gable roof. The Greek Revival style is evident in the symmetrical facade with a two-tiered entrance portico with two sets of superimposed fluted columns with Ionic pilasters. The floor plan is typical of early Tennessee plantations; one room deep, it has a central hall with staircase. The ceilings are nine feet high on the first floor and eight feet on the second. The ell contains only two rooms, as part was destroyed by fire.

Because of development in the area, the house was relocated in 1973 from its original site facing north to a site facing west on a residential street that was part of the original plantation. The restoration and moving exposed the early building techniques; hand-hewn timbers, mortice and tenon framing and blind bracing placed with large round wooden pegs. The corner posts are each made from one big log. The house is built of yellow poplar, cypress and white oak cut on the property.

The walls have split hickory laths that held plaster made with horsehair for strength. The bricks, hand-wrought iron hinges, screws and square nails were all made on the site. The floors are the original wide boards. The wainscoting was cut in wide pieces from large trees and the moldings illustrate frontier craftsmanship. Tools used in the building are still owned by the family.

Wilks Brooks donated the land for the Germantown Baptist Church in 1840. His son Joseph and wife Agnes later gave the land and lumber for the Baptist parsonage. They maintained a house in Germantown. They would drive the buggy to town on Saturday, purchasing supplies for the plantation and leaving them for the manager to pick up in a wagon. Then the Brooks stayed overnight to attend church services on Sunday. Agnes Brooks later lived in the Germantown house as a widow in 1898.

Joseph Brooks continued to buy land and added to his father's acreage, making trips to New Orleans to sell his cotton. When Joseph Brooks died in 1897, a funeral train was sent out from Memphis, stopped at Woodlawn Plantation, then bore the coffin and mourners to the burial in Elmwood Cemetary. The house is presently owned by the great-great-granddaughter of Wilks Brooks. ∎

Richwood

1 8 3 6 - 4 0

The land south of Germantown on which Richwood stands was home to the Indians for centuries. Shards and projectile points dating from the Paleo-Indian period (11,000 B.C. to 10,000 B.C.) as well as remnants of a late Indian hunting camp (after 1500 A.D.) have been found on the property. The first individual owner of the land was Co-She-Co, a Chickasaw. In 1832, when the Chickasaws began their move west to Oklahoma, each male over seventeen was alloted a specified parcel of land, the sales of which were to finance their move. In 1836, Mah-Ti-A-Cha, widow of Co-She-Co, sold the land to representatives of the United States government. On February 14, 1837, Daniel M. Riggs purchased the land, which at that time was presumed to be in DeSoto County, Mississippi.

The log house is thought to have been notched up between 1836 and 1840 during Riggs' ownership. It is a typical one-and-a-half story log house with central dogtrot. The sills, which rested on cedar-stump piers, measure more than twenty inches square and are of great length. The walls are braced with large timbers. No nails were used in building the frame. Spaces between the logs are filled with mud and slab chinking. Four windows are symmetrically placed in the front facade, but because of limited loft space under the roof, the upper windows are only half the height of the lower windows, creating an "eyebrow" effect. The exterior double flue chimneys on the gable ends of the house are hand-made brick covered by an early type of stucco; the upper stacks of the chimneys are freestanding as a precaution against fire.

Riggs owned the property for thirteen years. After a quick succession of several owners, Dr. Leonidas Polk Richmond purchased it in 1860. Richmond was born in North Carolina, raised in Marshall County, Mississippi, and graduated from the University of Pennsylvania Medical School in 1859, going back to North Carolina just long enough to marry. By the sixth of September, 1860, Richmond and his bride were living at the house he named Richwood. According to his descendants, it was during the short period before the Civil War that, family records say, he "paid an architect's passage from England" and the log house was changed to the appearance it has today. The craftsman enclosed the dogtrot and constructed steps to the upper story, added the weatherboarding, dentil molding and the Greek Revival front portico. The house was painted white with blinds flanking the windows; pillars, porch railing and bannisters are hand-made. The downstairs interior was covered with plaster of a pinkish cast, said to be mixed with blood and animal hair.

Dr. Richmond had no sooner started his medical practice — riding on horseback between Cordova and Olive Branch, Germantown and Forest Hill — than he left to serve for three years as a Confederate Army surgeon. After the war he returned to raise nine children at Richwood. A cotton gin and tenant houses stood behind the house, Dr. Richmond's office in a building in the front yard. The gin remained in operation until 1898 when a tornado destroyed it and felled every tree within a mile of the house.

During the yellow fever epidemic of 1878, Dr. Richmond stayed in his office for fear of contaminating his family. His meals were left on the steps, and he would not open the door until the person serving it had gone away from the office. His precautions were successful; he and his family were spared. He was an avid gardener and planted shrubs, flowers and pecan trees which can still be seen. Neighbors came to pick herbs from his medicinal garden, including strychnine and mosquito-repellent pennyroyal.

ABOVE:
Originally a log house built before 1840, Richwood received its present appearance before the Civil War.

AT RIGHT AND OPPOSITE:
The Mosby-Bennett house on Poplar between Memphis and Germantown.

Mosby-Bennett House

1 8 5 2

Located between Memphis and Germantown, the Mosby-Bennett house has watched a century's traffic on Poplar Pike. In the early 1980s it was restored and became a business office surrounded by a modern complex, its mellow charm reminding passers-by of an earlier day.

The ten room frame house was built as the center of a five thousand acre plantation in 1852 by Samuel and Joseph Mosby. It is a two-story rectangular structure with brick foundation, weatherboard siding and a slate-covered gable roof. Built in the Greek Revival style with a symmetrical facade, a decorated cornice, tall first floor windows, trabeated entrances, pilasters on the facade and at the corners of the house, it has Victorian decoration added after 1870.

The interior shows the adaptation of a plantation headquarters to the southen climate. Each floor has a central hall and four rooms. The ceilings are fourteen feet high and porches on each side can be reached through tall windows. The original decoration reflects the simplicity of the Greek Revival style.

When the Civil War started, Mrs. Mosby thought the house was too far in the country, so the Mosby families moved into Memphis, twelve miles away, for the duration of the war. They rented the house to William Lawrence Hall and his wife, who had moved from Kentucky because their son, Richard Robert Redford Hall, had joined Morgan's Kentucky Raiders, a Confederate cavalry unit, but the other members of the family were Union sympathizers. Robert Hall was wounded in the Battle of Vicksburg and sent to a Federal prison in Rockford, Illinois. He was to be exchanged for a Union prisoner in Richmond when the War ended, and he walked from Richmond to Memphis to join his family.

General Grant is said to have stopped at the house on his way to the Battle of Shiloh.

In 1870, the Mosbys sold the house and about 1,900 acres of land to George H. Bennett, a famous breeder of race horses, who installed his own racetrack on the property.

Mr. Bennett added a variety of Victorian details to the house: curvilinear bargeboards, porches on each side that feature bracketed posts, perforated railings and gingerbread trim, scrollwork above the window cornices and the peak of the facade's central gable. On the inside he added a heavily carved newel post to the stair, two marble mantlepieces, and picture rails. He also added a banquet hall in the basement and installed a Delco lighting system, an early electric generator.

At the rear of the house, Bennett built three gazebos, one of which still stands. It is twelve feet in diameter, octagonal with pointed arches.

In the early 1900s more alterations were made to the rear of the house. In 1979 it was sold to become the centerpiece of a modern office complex.

The combination of Victorian ornamentation and Greek Revival simplicity has produced a truly distinctive house. Its modern adaptation for commercial use preserves a charming Memphis landmark.   ∎

COLLIERVILLE

After the Chickasaw Cession in 1818, the land in west Tennessee was open for settlement and Shelby County was established on November 24, 1819. A settlement called Oak Grove grew on the highest land in the county along an old Indian Trace then called State Line Road, and later Poplar Pike.

The settlement was barely in Shelby County. In 1776 the thirty-fifth parallel north was declared the southern boundary of the state of North Carolina. In 1818 a survey established the boundary between Tennessee and Georgia; the line was extended westward by General Coffee and General Winchester in 1819. But the question of Tennessee's southern boundary was not finally settled for twenty years. A joint state commission met, and in 1837 Tennessee ratified the boundary which was accepted by Mississippi in 1838. The settlers were now firmly Tennesseans.

But where was the town to be? In 1833 the first post office was established in the area with Francis Halley as postmaster; it was just inside Fayette County. By 1837 the community had solidified and the post office was moved across the line into Shelby County with John W. Koen as postmaster, and christened Collierville.

The name comes from Jesse R. Collier who stayed in Shelby County just long enough to leave his name. In the 1830 census he was a resident of Fayette County; in 1840 he was located in the southeast corner of Shelby County; and by 1856 he had moved on to Tippah County, Mississippi. Tradition says he was a storekeeper; he was probably a land speculator.

The town of Collierville was developing in the 1840s. The earliest settlers included Adams, Ramseys, Bloodworths, Youngs, and Bounds. The town was laid out on land belonging to Floyd, Adams and Tharp. Located on the crossroads of main roads into Mississippi, Memphis and east into Tennessee, it was an agricultural and trading center.

The Memphis and LaGrange Railroad was chartered in 1835 but got off to a slow start. By 1842 only a few miles of track had been laid, from Memphis east as far as Colonel Eppy White's station. In 1850 the Memphis and Charleston Railroad bought the charter, and the first train came through Collierville in 1852. It was a great event! A resident near Marley's Crossing wrote:

> The people from all directions living in the country came in to see the first train come by. I had twenty people spend the day with me. Long before the train was scheduled to arrive, the citizens lined the area along the tracks, hitching their horses to tree limbs and fences. Finally the train with much huffing and blowing and smoke boiling out of a funnel-shaped smokestack, came in sight through the cut near Mrs. B. M. Cowan's home. Most of the people were literally scared out of their wits. Children ran into the woods and many people ran, too; some actually fell down on the ground and covered their faces.
> *(quoted in Parr, "History of Collierville,"* Collierville Herald *special edition, 1981)*

Before the railroad, the normal means of getting to Memphis twenty-four miles away was an overnight wagon trip, later on a plank road. There had been irregular service on the Wolf River, but it was a great day when the first three bales of Collierville cotton were shipped by rail on October 30, 1852. Peter Adams and his family gave two acres of land for the first depot. By 1857 the railroad reached from Charleston to Memphis, connecting the Atlantic with the Mississippi. The completion of the line was celebrated with the "wedding of the waters" when Atlantic seawater was poured into the Mississippi River with great fanfare. The railroad issued a guidebook for its passengers that identified Collierville as a town of two hundred and fifty inhabitants, occupying a high position on the ridge twenty-four miles from Memphis. The fare between the two towns was seventy-five cents.

Collierville grew fast in the next decade and at the coming of the Civil War had a population of five hundred. It was incorporated in 1857 with Richard Ramsey as mayor, but ceased to function as a town after a short time because of the disruptions and damages of the war.

As war approached, the citizens of Collierville began to prepare. A troop called the Wigfall Grays (named in honor of Senator Wigfall of Texas who had delivered a fiery speech in defense of the South) was organized on April 15, 1861, with eighty members. The ladies of Collierville met at the Methodist Church to sew uniforms for the soldiers. On the evening of Saturday, May 11, orders were received for the troops to report to Germantown on the thirteenth, and the ladies sewed all day Sunday to finish the last four uniforms. As the troops assembled early on the morning of Monday, May 13, a beautiful silk flag, also sewn by the ladies, was presented by Miss Koen to the officer in charge, Lieutenant Hammond. The Wigfall Grays served at Shiloh, Chickamauga, Atlanta, Adairsville, Missionary Ridge, and other battles as Company C of the Fourth Tennessee Infantry.

There were several skirmishes at Collierville as Union troops had a fortification and a hospital there. In April of 1862 word came of the bloody battle at Shiloh. The ladies brought blankets, sheets and even their table linens to make into bandages as the train brought some of the wounded to be cared for at Collierville.

An engagement that came to be known as the Battle of Collierville occured in 1863. General William Tecumseh Sherman left Union headquarters in Memphis on the morning of October 11, bound for Corinth, Mississippi, in the first stage of his march to the sea. His train passed a division of Union soldiers on foot at Germantown. About noon the train reached Collierville, where the troops of Confederate General James R. Chalmers were attacking a Federal encampment. Sherman was able to wire for reinforcements and the troops they had passed at Germantown were put to marching double time.

Bloody fighting ensued, the Confederates attacking the train and making off with Sherman's favorite horse, Dolly, and his saber, among other things. General Sherman wrote:

> All the houses near, that could give shelter to the enemy, were ordered to be set on fire, and the men were instructed to keep well under cover and to reserve their fire for the assault which seemed inevitable. . . The enemy closed down on us several times, and got possession of the rear of our train, from which they succeeded in getting five of our horses, among them my favorite mare Dolly; but our men were cool and practiced shots (with great experience acquired at Vicksburg) and drove them back. With this artillery they knocked to pieces our locomotive and several of the cars, and set fire to the train. . . Colonel Audenreid, aide-de-camp, was provoked to find that his valise of nice shirts had been used to kindle the fire.
>
> *Sherman's* Memoirs,
> *Vol. I, pp. 379-381*

The fighting had gone on for about four hours when the Union reinforcements arrived and the Confederates were forced to scatter. J. S. Hooper, a Confederate soldier in the battle, wrote, "Our boys raided Sherman's commissary car and paused to eat and drink cake and wine while the blue whistlers were speeding past their ears." He quotes a soldiers' ditty commemorating the event:

> General Chalmers, the gallant and gay,
> Made a raid in Tennessee,
> Captured Sherman's horse, sword and saddle
> Then made away for other prey.
> *(quoted in "This is Collierville," special edition
> of* Collierville Herald, *1981)*

But the battle was not at all gallant and gay; it was bloody and disastrous for the town of Collierville The casualties were high and the town was severely damaged. Thus the beginning of Sherman's infamous march to the sea.

After the war the town had to rebuild. In 1867 and 1868 the bodies of fifty known and seventy-six unknown Federal soldiers were removed for burial in National Cemetery in Memphis. The original eighty Wigfall Grays had added thirty-one recruits. Of these one hundred and eleven, only thirty-four names were on the company rolls at the end of the war. Sixteen were killed in battle, sixteen died of wounds or sickness, sixteen were discharged because of wounds or sickness, fifteen deserted (five joined the Union and one joined General Forrest), twelve were transferred, and one hired a substitute who was killed in the war.

After the war, Harrison Irby and Dr. Virginius Leake bought ninety acres, divided it into lots and sold them. This moved the town nearer to the railroad from its earlier location on the State Line Road. Irby served as magistrate and constable and was deputy sheriff several times. The town was beginning to come back to life.

In 1870 the town was incorporated with J. B. Abington as mayor. There were four churches: Baptist, Methodist, Presbyterian and Christian. In 1872 a plot of land was fenced in and deer and peacocks were put into Collierville's first park. A bandstand for public concerts was built in 1876 and a dance was held to celebrate.

Collierville escaped the yellow fever epidemics of the early 1870s, but 1878 proved disastrous. On August 15, 1878, a public quarantine was announced: no freight or passengers by rail or river were to be allowed to unload at Collierville. Trains were not allowed to stop and the roads were all patrolled. The town was said to smell to high heaven because the streets were poured with sulphur in an attempt to kill the unknown plague.

Despite these precautions the epidemic raged. There were one hundred and thirty-five cases reported and fifty-seven deaths. In September fifty-one families had evacuated and others were leaving. People were terrified, and almost no household was spared. Every day at five o'clock the men of the town gathered at the depot for prayer and to take an inventory of who was missing since the day before. The mayor, the town marshall and several doctors were among the casualties. Finally, on October 28, the frost came. The plague was over and people could return home.

The town continued to be a prosperous and stable community, a center for the commerce of the region. In 1874, Dr. E. K. Leake organized a baseball team, the "Collierville Athletics," that toured the South. Spelling bees were an important community event. In 1879 the *Collierville Herald* was first published. By 1886, Collierville was the second town in the county with twelve hundred inhabitants. The Episcopal Church was built in 1890, the same year the Collierville Bank was organized. In the 1890s horse racing and a bicycle club were popular entertainments.

Collierville is the only town in Shelby County with a public square at its center, a living symbol of its spirit of community and a tradition of the South. ■

DeLoach House 1840s

The two-story frame house on the north side of Poplar Pike west of Collierville has had many owners. It has a one-story porch with iron posts, tall windows on the first floor and irregular "eyebrow" windows on the second floor, above the porch. There are four brick chimneys.

The house was built in the 1840s by Thomas Hill Peters. During the Civil War it was lived in by Josiah DeLoach, who entertained General Grant there in 1862. DeLoach had been married to Huldah Dean, and they had a son, William. She died in 1847, and that same year he married Olivia Hill in Marshall County, Mississippi. She was the widow of Duncan Hill, a school teacher who had educated himself as a physician and who left a sizable estate upon his death in 1844. He also left ten children, including Napolean Hill (important in the development of South Memphis), and three other sons, Duncan, Jerome and Harry.

General Grant's *Personal Memoirs* for June 23, 1862, say:

> The road from LaGrange to Memphis was very warm, even for that latitude and season. . . Before noon we arrived within 20 miles of Memphis. At that point I saw a very comfortable looking white-haired gentleman seated at the front of his house, a little distance from the road. I let my staff and escort ride ahead while I halted and, for an excuse, asked for a glass of water. I was invited at once to dismount and come in. . . The gentleman with whom I had stopped was a Mr. DeLoche, a man loyal to the Union. He had not pressed me to tarry longer with him because in the early part of my visit a neighbor, a Dr. Smith, had called and, on being presented to me, backed off the porch as if something had hit him.

Tradition says that while Grant was at the house, word came that Confederate troops were approaching and that DeLoach helped Grant escape. Grant himself did not remember it that way. Certainly Confederates were in the neighborhood and certainly Grant did make it to Memphis, but probably without DeLoach's help. A day or two later, DeLoach called upon Grant at his headquarters in Memphis to apologize for his incivility. Grant had discovered from a cattle drover that he had had a narrow escape from Confederate General Jackson. DeLoach was appointed postmaster at Memphis after the war by Grant.

DeLoach had both a son and stepsons serving in the Confederate army. The story goes that he told General Grant that though he supported the Union, he would also support his sons, and General Grant replied, "Sir, you would be an unnatural parent if it were not so."

DeLoach is also quoted as saying to his stepson on his deathbed, "Harry, tell Dr. Rogers I'm not afraid to die because I've never once voted the Democratic party."

Jerome Hill inherited the house and sold it to a Mr. Bassett, who later sold it to Monroe Cartwright, whose grandson, Monroe Frank, built a house nearby to the east. The grandfather was called Mon and the grandson Roe to avoid confusion. ■

Virginius Leake House

1840s

Samuel Leake and his brother Richard brought their families to Tennessee from Goochland County, Virginia, in the 1830s and settled in the Morning Sun Community, near what is presently Eads. The first post office there was called Leakeville, and Samuel Leake was its postmaster. His son, Virginius, was born in 1822, before the family moved to Tennessee. He became a doctor, and it is he, along with Harrison Irby, who sold lots and developed Collierville after the Civil War.

In the 1840s Virginius Leake built a large plantation house on the Collierville-Arlington Road of wood cut on his four hundred and ninety-eight acre farm. It is a handsome two-story central hall plan with an impressive portico supported by four octagonal columns. The windows have triangular lintels, and the doors on both floors have sidelights and transoms. A balcony with square posts and a spindle railing stretches over the entrance under the portico. An unusual scalloped molding decorates the eaves and the portico.

Dr. Leake and his three sons attended Virginia Military Institute. His daughter Martha Ellen married Dr. Maurice Fletcher and inherited the house. His sons were Dr. Elgin Leake, organizer of Collierville's first baseball team and its public water company; Dr. Millard Fillmore Leake, a Methodist minister and principal of Collierville Male Academy; and Tingnal H. Leake, who studied to be a lawyer, but according to the family, "was too honest and had to find another way to make a living" and became a machinist instead.

■

ABOVE:
*The Davis-Porter house
near Collierville is
typical of ante-bellum
plantation architecture.*

Davis-Porter House

1850s

The land on which the Davis-Porter house stands, west of Collierville, was sold by a female Chickasaw Indian, She-Mi-O-Kay, to William Craine in April, 1836. Craine in turn sold the land to William Cranfield, Trustee for four Freeman children in 1841. By the time the land was sold again, a house had been built, but it is uncertain exactly where. In 1857, two hundred and twenty-one acres were conveyed to Andrew Taylor, a descendent of Zachary Taylor, and a large landowner in the area. Andrew Taylor lived in a large frame plantation home to the west of the Davis-Porter home, but that house burned many years ago.

Taylor gave each of his children land when they mar-ried, and this parcel went to his daughter, Laura Theresa, upon her marriage to Charles R. Davis in 1856. The Davises may have built the home about that time. A son, Charles Robert, was born there in 1866 and inherited the house in 1891. He served in the Tennessee Legislature and raised a family on the land. Three generations of Davises lived there until it was sold before the Second World War. The house stood empty for some years, but has been restored.

It is a typical white frame plantation house with a simple two-story portico supported by four square columns. Tall double doors with sidelights center the front facade on each floor, with a wrought iron balcony under the portico. The house has a standing seam metal roof and a center hall plan. ■

Fleming Place

South of Collierville stands a handsome two-story white frame house with a Greek Revival portico that is typical of the plantation architecture of the region. The cornice and portico have ornamental brackets across the front, which contrast with the undecorated severity of the back and sides. Tall narrow windows are grouped in pairs on either side of the entrance. The portico is supported by tall fluted columns and outlined by pilasters. A wrought iron balcony is over the entrance; the doors on both floors have squared sidelights and transoms.

Inside is a central hall with square rooms on either side and a two-story ell at the back. Each room has a fireplace with the original mantel. The stairway in the front hall has a walnut balustrade, and there is also a "daughters stairway," leading from the back bedroom upstairs down into the master bedroom - an early way of chaperoning the unmarried daughters. The floors are random-width long leaf pine and there are boxed wooden cornices over the windows. Downstairs the ceilings are twelve feet high and upstairs ten feet. The interior doors have six panels with deep molding.

The land on which the house is built was part of three sections (one thousand nine hundred and twenty acres) ceded to an Indian, Nick-e-Yea under an 1834 treaty between the United States and the Chickasaw Nation. Nick-e-Yea sold the land to Edward McGehee for four thousand dollars in 1836. In 1849, John Fleming, a South Carolinian of Irish descent who was an elder in the nearby Salem Presbyterian Church, bought one section and between 1855 and 1860, built his home on a rise.

Fleming had married Eliza Moseley in 1840, and they had a son, Samuel, and a daughter, Nancy, who married J. Boyce Farley. Eliza Fleming died in 1860, and John Fleming married Mrs. Fannie Gooch in 1864. She died the next year, and he married again in 1867 to Mrs. A. B. Sullivan.

Samuel Fleming enlisted in the Confederate Army at the age of eighteen and was a prisoner of war at Rock Island, Illinois, for sixteen months.

The Hamner family liked the Fleming house so much that they built one like it on Center Street in Collierville after the Civil War, but that house burned in the twentieth century.

During the yellow fever epidemic of 1878, Dr. and Mrs. A. S. Stratton moved their family (and their piano) from Collierville to the Fleming place to escape the fever. ∎

ABOVE:
*The Fleming house near
Collierville was built
between 1855 and 1860.*

ABOVE:
The Stratton-Owen house in Collierville is plantation-style on a smaller scale for a town lot.

Stratton-Owen Place 1870

Dr. A. S. Stratton was born in Athol, Massachusetts, in 1820, the son of a farmer and shoemaker. In 1845 he moved to Como, Mississippi, where he read medicine, then graduated from the Memphis Medical College in 1848. Soon after he moved to Collierville, where, in addition to practicing medicine, he was involved in a variety of mercantile ventures. His first firm was Moore and Stratton; later he sold goods in Centerville, Mississippi; still later he was a partner with E. G. Kindred, and then with J. T. Biggs for sixteen years. In 1884 he went into partnership with his son-in-law, Turner Humphreys, as Stratton and Humphreys.

In 1849, Dr. Stratton married Mary Elizabeth Chamberlain of Sharon, Connecticut, whose brothers were missionaries and educators. They had one daughter, Mary Eudora, who married Turner Humphreys. Years later, a descendent, wondering about the adventuresome young woman who had settled so far from her home, asked how Grandmother Stratton had come alone from Connecticut to Tennessee. The reply was, "Elizabeth, the woods were full of Yankee school-teachers."

While Dr. Stratton pursued his medical practice and his various business enterprises, Mrs. Stratton taught school in a small building behind their house. Dr. Stratton was a Presbyterian and a Democrat and must have been a real estate speculator, too, for his name is connected with several houses in Collierville. His great-granddaughter still lives in the house on Natchez in which he lived in 1868.

About 1870 the Strattons moved to a house on Rowlett, but only lived there a short time before selling it in 1873. Since then it has had many owners.

The house is a typical two-story house with a Greek Revival portico supported by two octagonal columns with half-octagon pilasters on either side of the entrance. A balcony with a carved wooden railing is over the entrance and the pediment is decorated by a scrolled ventilation grill. It has a central hall plan with one room on each side and a one-story ell in back. ∎

AT RIGHT:
*A variety of decoration
ornaments the building
built in 1886 for the
Collierville Presbyterian
Church.*

Collierville

1 8 8 6

Presbyterian Church

The Presbyterian congregation was organized in 1844 with twenty-one members as Salem Presbyterian Church. At first they were located two miles south of town on Byhalia Road. In the 1870s the congregation moved into Collierville and shared the Methodist meeting house until 1886, when they built a church on Walnut Street. The building still stands although the congregation moved to a larger modern building in 1965.

The building on Walnut Street is a rectangular white frame building with four windows on each side. The windows are set into rectangular openings but have stained glass in the shape of a pointed arch. The east facade has no windows and tall double doors under a stained glass transom. A small square steeple with louvers is above the entrance. Under the eaves is a variety of decoration; horizontal panelling, two kinds of sunburst carving and an ornamental grill, relieving the simplicity of the building. ■

Nolley House

1866-67

One of the oldest homes in Collierville was built by the first post-Civil War mayor, James B. Abington. He had acquired land from Olsey Bail Armour north of town, and in 1866 and 1867 built a house with two rooms on either side of a dogtrot. Abington probably never lived in the house for in 1867 he sold it to a returning Civil War prisoner and it has been in that family ever since.

The inside was finished when they moved in. In 1928 they added rooms to the back and closed in the dogtrot, but the original wood siding remains on the exterior. ∎

ABOVE:
The Nolley house near Collierville originally had a dogtrot.

AT LEFT:
The Humphreys house in Collierville has Gay Nineties gingerbread trim.

Humphreys House

1890

An unusual house at the corner of Natchez and Mt. Pleasant has a quaint charm. The two wings sit at an angle to each other with a triangular porch over the entrance in the angle. A steeply pointed gable centers the porch. The porch has paired piers with gingerbread trim, and more gingerbread and lattice work on the back porch.

Turner Humphreys built the house in the 1890s, but probably intended it for rental rather than his residence. He was married to Mary Eudora Stratton, daughter of Dr. A. S. Stratton, and Humphreys was a partner with his father-in-law in the firm of Stratton and Humphreys. He was also an elder in the Presbyterian Church. ∎

St. Andrew's Episcopal Church

1890

As Collierville rebuilt itself upon the ashes after the destruction of the Civil War, there were several churches built, representing different denominations. There were no more than two or three families of the Episcopal faith, certainly not enough to call a congregation. But from these small beginnings came St. Andrew's Episcopal Church. The first services were held in the parlor of the home of Mary Louise and Joseph H. Mangum. Bishop Greene of Mississippi, the Reverend George White of Calvary Church in Memphis, Bishop Pierce of Arkansas and Bishop Quintard, who had been a chaplin in the Confederate Army and a comrade of Mr. Mangum's, all visited to hold services for the little flock.

In 1875 Miss Anna Holden came to Collierville as a teacher at Bellevue College. The next year she attended the Diocesan Convention meeting in Memphis, where she met an old friend, the Reverend W. C. Gray of Bolivar, Tennessee, who agreed to hold regular services for the faithful few Episcopalians in Collierville. The services were held in the College, the Mangum home, the John Holden home and in the Christian Church building.

About 1881 this determined lady opened her own school, Holden's Seminary. For about eight years monthly church services were held there, with Sunday School every Sunday. Undeterred by their small numbers, seven earnest women began a movement to build an Episcopal Church in Collierville. They mailed thousands of little red brick cards to the Episcopal congregations around the country soliciting funds; each card had fifty bricks at ten cents each. Contributions came from all over the United States. Bazaars were held, attracting people from LaGrange, Somerville, Holly Springs and Memphis. Finally, on April 22, 1890, Bishop Quintard of Tennessee laid the cornerstone of the new building. The Bishop himself donated the side windows which he had obtained while attending the Lambeth Conference in London. He returned to consecrate the church in 1891.

The church is built of warm red brick in a romantic Gothic-revival style with steeply pitched roof, pointed-arch windows on either side between four plaster-topped brick buttresses. Stained glass windows on the sides and over the altar and over the twelve foot tall entrance doors were given as memorials. ∎

The land along the southwestern border of Shelby County was a lonely wilderness of swampy bottoms of cypress trees and canebrakes. Because of the low-lying swampy nature of the land it was settled later than the rest of the county. But after the Indian treaties of the 1830s when the Choctaws and then the Chickasaws were moved west, settlers began to move in. Each Indian male and each unmarried female over twenty was granted land which was sold to the white settlers. So the early deeds bear names such as Luke Measles and Ton Tubby.

As early as 1819 Benjamin and Daniel Hilderbrand came twice a year from Mississippi to trade in the area. Other early settlers were named Person, Edmonson, Edminston, Morgan, Holmes, Isbell, Plunkett, Nelson, Davis, Farrow, and Raines. In 1843 the first school was established on the property of Daniel Hilderbrand, and in 1844, the first church, a Presbyterian congregation, was organized, soon followed by the Baptists and the Methodists. Permanent settlers replaced land speculators and the area became a friendly rural community.

In 1846 the Memphis and Grenada Railroad (now the Illinois Central) was chartered, but nothing much happened until Colonel Francis M. White of Como, Mississippi, took over. Under his leadership, financing and rail-laying progressed and the line reached Hernando in 1856. The area in south Shelby County became known as White's Station or White's Haven for him.

Whitehaven retained its peaceful rural character until the late 1930s, when urban development began and the area mushroomed into a busy part of the city of Memphis. ∎

Hale House 1870s

The main road from the Mississippi delta into Memphis was once bordered with handsome farms and homes. Today Highway 51 passes through shopping malls, schools, churches, fast food shops, and busloads of tourists arriving at the home of Elvis Presley. The last remnant of nineteenth century Whitehaven, the Hale House, stands almost upon the Mississippi border.

The house is a one-story white clapboard cottage set back from the highway amid old cedar trees and tall oaks, one of which has an eighteen foot circumference. It was built in the late 1870s as a yellow fever refuge, removed from the stricken city of Memphis. In the early 1880s, the house and surrounding land were acquired by George R. Hale, whose family was among the early settlers of the Whitehaven area. George R. Hale was born in 1856 near Oxford, Mississippi, and had a dairy and truck farm in Whitehaven, where he was a charter member of the Baptist Church. His grandson lives in the house today.

The house originally consisted of two rooms and a

central hall with fourteen foot ceilings plus a two-room ell. The floors are three-fourths inch by four inches poplar tongue-in-groove boards, and most of the woodwork is poplar. A porch stretches across most of the front with square pilasters on either side of the entrance. The original four large square pillars have been replaced with smaller round ones. The entrance door has a transom and the original brass door bell. ∎

AT LEFT:
*The Hilderbrand house
was built around 1838
by some of the earliest
settlers in Whitehaven.*

Hilderbrand House

1838

In the eighteenth century the Hilderbrand family lived in the southwestern corner of Pennsylvania which was disputed territory between Virginia and Pennsylvania. Around 1796 the sons of Judge Abraham Hildebrand left for the western territories. Some settled in St. Louis-St. Genevieve counties in Missouri and others lived around Natchez, Mississippi. One Ben Hildebrand and his brother Daniel came about twice a year to the Chickasaw Bluff to trade with the Indians, living in a log cabin located near Millbranch and Shelby Drive during their trading expeditions. Family lore says that as early as 1819 they applied for a seven thousand acre grant of land. They were offered land near today's court house for forty cents an acre, but chose land south near their trading cabin although it was eighty cents an acre.

But for some reason the grant was not issued for some years. Finally, after payment of $1,280 to a Chickasaw Indian name Ton Tubby, Benjamin A. Hilderbrand received a deed signed by President Martin Van Buren in 1838. The Benjamin Hilderbrand who took possession was probably a son of the trader; his tombstone in Edmondson Chapel Cemetary gives his birth as July 25, 1806, and his death as December 20, 1879.

In 1833, this Benjamin Hilderbrand married Susan Robertson with Isaac Rawlings as acting Justice of the Peace. Hilderbrand operated a store, grist mill and cotton gin along Millbranch Road and farmed land which spread from the Mississippi line to today's Airways Boulevard. Near what is now Airways, he built his house, a plantation-style built of hand-hewn hickory logs pegged together, with a center hall plan and a veranda with two-story square columns facing east. The house was built around 1838. In the 1850 Shelby County Census Benjamin Hilderbrand's real estate was listed as having a value of $10,000 and he and his wife, a niece, two daughters and four sons were all named as residents. His descendent married the daughter of Edward Elam of the Elam Homestead. ∎

AFTERWORD

HISTORIC PRESERVATION:
Our Past, Present and Future

by Eleanor D. Hughes

It has taken twenty-five years to span the cycle, but historic preservation is coming of age in Memphis and Shelby County. The mid-'50s era of Urban Renewal and the "new is better" concept has become an "adaptive re-use" and restoration philosophy.

Many influences have brought us to this point — downtown revitalization, rising construction costs, a new interest in our past, and legislation offering tax incentives and freezes. Restored, converted and back on our tax rolls are previously empty and rapidly deteriorating warehouses, schools, commercial buildings and residential structures.

Restoration and preservation are a philosophy that values all types of architecture. From the grand Victorian mansions on Adams and palatial homes in Collierville, to the small frame dwellings in Greenlaw and Arlington, types of architecture that depict our heritage and the people who helped build this area are represented.

Concern and support for this movement are still needed for future direction, or our legacy of past design, architecture and methods of construction will be gone. To know where we are going and to plan for the future we must look back at our past and treat it with the respect and dignity it deserves.

ARCHITECTURAL
GLOSSARY

STYLES

Adam Style — characterized by straight lines, surface decoration, and use of conventional design such as festooned garlands and medallions. Named for the Adam brothers, 18th century English architects.

Art Deco — a decorative style characterized by sharp angular or zigzag surface forms and ornaments; stimulated by the Paris Exposition of 1925 and widely used in skyscraper designs of the 1930s.

Carpenter Gothic — simplified and informal version of Gothic Revival with elements fabricated by craftsmen.

Federal — America's first style, named in honor of the new Republic (1789); it uses classical parts to articulate entrances, windows and cornices, and gambrel roofs with dormers. Emphasizes simplicity and clarity.

French Victorian (also Second Empire or Mansard) — characterized by the use of mansard (double pitched) roofs, the stress of dimensionality by projecting and receding surfaces in the form of central and end pavillions, towers, dormers and detailed chimneys. Emphasized height, frequently asymmetrical. The name Second Empire comes from the reign of Napoleon III of France.

Gothic Revival — characterized by medieval features such as pointed arches, steep gable roofs, battlements, pinnacles, vaulting, window tracery, and buttresses. Particularly seen in church architecture.

Greek Revival — characterized by classically detailed columns and pilasters in the Greek style in symmetrical arrangement, triangular pediments and columned porticos. Greek forms were considered symbolic of democracy.

Italianate — characterized by the rounding of sharp points and arches of true Gothic. Uses tall narrow windows with segmentally arched or flat heads. Uses large cornices and oversized metal brackets and window heads.

Neo-Classic — the last phase of European classicism in late 18th and 19th century. Characterized by monumentality, strict use of the orders and sparing application of ornament.

Romanesque — characterized by use of the round arch and vault, decorative arcades, substitution of piers for columns and profuse ornament.

Richardsonian Romanesque — characterized by massive rock faced masonry on a basically round-arched Romanesque style. Emphasis on structural elements such as arches, piers and deeply recessed windows. Overall effect of massive solid structure. Named for American architect Henry Hobson Richardson.

Queen Anne — characterized by contrast and variety. Mixture of materials, bold colors and ornamentation. Assymetry emphasized, as in towers, turrets and multiple roofs. Frequent use of stained and leaded glass.

Vernacular — the common building style of a period or place.

ARCHITECTURAL TERMS

acanthus — an architectural ornament patterned after the leaves of the acanthus plant, with large, jagged-edged leaves; the ornament usually forms the lower portions of the Corinthian capital.

apse — a semi-circular or polygonal, usually domed, projection of a building, especially the altar or east end of a church.

arcade — a series of arches supported on piers or columns.

arch — in masonry construction, a method of spanning an opening in a wall by a series of bricks or stones arranged in a curved configuration, so as to be self-supporting.

architrave — the molding around a door or window.

ashlar — masonry of squared stones laid in regular courses.

balustrade — a handrail or parapet.

bargeboard — inclined projecting boards placed at the gable of a building and hiding the horizontal timbers of the roof.

battlement — a parapet built on top of a wall, with indentations for defense or decoration.

bay — the internal compartments of a building marked by divisions on the side walls.

bay window — a window projecting outward beyond the face of a wall.

beveled (bevel) — a sloping surface, usually on an edge.

bracket — a simple rigid structure in the shape of an inverted L, one arm of which is fixed to a vertical surface, with the other projecting horizontally to support a shelf, roof, or other weight.

bull's eye window — a circular window.

bungalow — a small cottage, usually one story.

buttress — a structure, usually brick or stone, built against a wall for support or reinforcement.

capital — the top part, or head, of a pillar or column.

casement — a window sash opening on hinges.

cast iron — formed of iron that has been cast, containing a higher percentage of carbon than wrought iron.

chancel — the space around the altar of a church for the clergy and choir, often enclosed by a railing.

chinking — material used for filling a chink in a wall.

clapboard — exterior wood siding, consisting of horizontal overlapping boards. Sometimes called weatherboard.

console — a decorative bracket for supporting a cornice, shelf, bust or other object.

corbel — a bracket of stone, wood, brick or other building material, projecting from the face of a wall and generally used to support a cornice or an arch.

cornice — the uppermost section of a classical entablature.

course — in brickwork, a single horizontal row of bricks.

crenallation — the crown of a medieval fortification, later used as decoration, with notched or indented battlements.

cross gable — a gable which is set parallel to the ridge of the roof.

cruciform — cross-shaped.

cupola — a small structure, usually domed, surmounting a roof.

curvilinear — formed or characterized by curved lines.

dentil — one of a series of small rectangular blocks forming a molding or projection beneath a cornice.

dogtrot — plan of two parts separated by a breezeway, all under a common roof. This evolved into the central hall with rooms opening on either side. Usually found in early log cabins.

dormer — a small gable in a pitched roof, usually housing a window.

eave — the overhanging edge of a roof.

encaustic — pertaining to a painting process in which colored beeswax is applied and fixed with heat.

entablature — the upper part of an order of architecture, between the capitals of the columns and the roof. Comprises: architrave
    frieze
    cornice

etagere — a series of open shelves.

eyebrow windows — upper windows that are half the height of those below.

facade — the outside face of a building.

finial — an ornament placed at the peak of an arch or gable.

fluting — the vertical channeling on the shaft of a column or pilaster.

french window — a tall window opening in two leaves like a folding door.

fresco — painting by pressing colors dissolved in water into fresh plaster, or by painting colors onto fresh plaster so as to have the color absorbed into the plaster.

fretwork — ornamental work consisting of interlacing parts especially when the design is formed by perforation.

frieze — a decorative horizontal band, as along the upper part of a wall in a room; or, in a classical entablature, between the architrave and the cornice.

gable — the triangular shape formed by the enclosing lines of a sloping roof.

gallery — (1) a covered space for walking in, with one side open, or (2) a platform projecting from the wall of a building, or (3) a long upstairs room, or (4) a room used for the display of art, or (5) a separate building for the same purpose.

galvanized iron — a coating against corrosion.

galvanized tin — a coating against corrosion.

gargoyle — a waterspout usually designed as a grotesque animal; in medieval buildings, a stone spout, delivering water downwards and outwards from a parapet gutter, the end of the gargoyle was often carved to represent grotesque heads or beasts.

gazebo — a garden pavilion; usually a summer-house at the end of a garden terrace, commanding a view.

gingerbread — the highly decorative woodwork applied to Gingerbread style houses, or the like.

Greek key — ornamentation of continuous lines arranged in rectangular forms.

header — a brick or stone laid so that the longest dimension is in the thickness of the wall, at rigid angles to its length, and only the end appears on the face.

herringbone — an arrangement of facing in diagonal patterns for decorative purposes, as in herringbone brickwork.

hip roof — roof with sloping ends and sloping sides.

hood molds — a roof-like projecting cover over a niche, window, door, etc.; sometimes called canopy.

horseshoe arch — largely used in Muslim architecture, may be either the round horseshoe or Moorish arch, or the pointed horseshoe.

jerkinhead — the end of a roof when it is formed into a shape intermediate between a gable and a hip.

jigsaw brackets — scrolled decoration cut with a jigsaw.

keystone — the central wedge-shaped stone at the summit of an arch that locks the others together.

lath — a narrow strip of wood.

lattice — a framework of interlacing laths.

leaded glass — window glass composed of small individual panes separated by thin beads of lead, often arranged in a decorative pattern.

lintel — horizontal structural member across the top of a door or window opening.

lotus leaf capital — top of column made to look like lotus leaves.

mansard roof — a roof having two slopes on all four sides, the lower slope almost vertical. Named after French architect Francois Mansard.

mantel — originally the hoodlike masonry structure that supported a chimney's fireplace, later used as either the whole framework around a fireplace or its overhanging shelf.

medallion — in architecture, a circular or oval plaque.

mezzanine — a low story between two stories of greater height.

modillion — a small ornamental bracket, used in rows under the corona of a cornice.

mortise and tenon — a tenon, the shaped projection on a piece of wood, is set in a mortise, a hole or slot of identical size.

molding — an embellishment in strip form used to decorate a surface or cover a joint.

mosaic — a picture or decorative design made by setting small colored pieces, such as tile or glass, in mortar.

nave — the central part of a church, often with aisles.

newel post — a post supporting one end of a handrail on a flight of stairs.

niche — an ornamental recess in a wall.

orders — a column with its base and capital together with the entablature it supports:
  Doric — capital consists of plain molding, no base

Ionic — scroll-like capital, molded base
Corinthian — capital of stylized acanthus leaves

ornament — detail, such as molding or carving, which is added to a building for expressive or decorative purposes.

parquet — hardwood, thin and in small pieces, that form a patterned floor veneer.

pediment — the triangular face of a gable placed over a door, window or porch.

permastone veneer — process in which a finish is applied to give the appearance of stone.

piano box plan — floor plan in the shape of a "U", centered by a recessed porch, reminiscent of the shape of boxed pianos of the 19th century.

pier — an independent solid mass of stone, brick, or concrete which supports a vertical load or the thrust of an arch.

pierced siding — decorated with perforations.

pilaster — a column which is partially attached or embedded in the face of a wall.

pinnacle — a small turret or spire on a roof or buttress.

porte cochere — a large porch to shelter persons alighting from a carriage outside the entrance of a building.

portico — a colonnaded porch forming the entrance to a building.

pulpit — an elevated platform, lectern, or stand used in preaching or conducting a religious service.

pyramidal — having the shape of a pyramid.

quoin — dressed or emphasized stones set at the corner of a building in a regular vertical pattern.

reeding — a convex decorative molding having parallel strips resembling thin reeds.

riser — the vertical part of a stairstep.

rostrum — a dais, platform, or similar raised place for public speaking.

rotunda — a large and high circular hall, especially one surmounted by a dome.

sconce — a decorative wall bracket for candles or lights.

scrollwork — carved in the form of a scroll of paper.

segmentally arched — any round headed arch that is only a segment of a circle; less than a semi-circle.

shingle — thin pieces of wood or other material set in overlapping rows to cover the roofs and sides of houses.

shiplap siding — interlocking boards, each lapped behind another's joint, usually with a space between to leave a designed shadow.

shutter — a hinged cover or screen for a window, usually fitted with louvers.

side light — a framed area of fixed glass alongside a door or window opening.

skylight — an overhead window admitting daylight.

slate — a rock from schist that splits into leaflike layers, usable in its natural form for walkways, firehearths and as an alternate for shingles.

spandrel — the triangular space enclosed by the curve of an arch, a vertical line from its springing and a horizontal line through its apex.

spire — a formation of structure that tapers to a point at the top, as a steeple.

springer — the bottom stone of an arch resting on the uppermost part of a column or pillar supporting an arch.

square corner notching — log building technique where logs do not protrude beyond each other and form a square corner.

standing seam — in metal roofing, a type of seam between adjacent sheets of material made by turning up the edges of two adjacent sheets and then folding them over.

steeple — a tall tower surmounted by a spire.

stucco — plaster used on exterior walls that may be finished in a variety of colors and textures.

stylized — a manner, mode or fashion of building practiced at any one period, and distinguished by certain characteristics of general design, construction and ornament.

terra cotta — cast and fired clay masonry, harder in quality than brick.

tower — any lofty structure, other than a dome, rising above the general roof level of a building, for purposes of defense, observation or decoration.

trabeated — having horizontal beams or lintels rather than arches.

transom — a small hinged window above a door or window.

triglyph — a member of a Doric frieze consisting of three incised vertical elements, separating square spaces.

turret — a small ornamental tower, usually at the corner of a building.

vaulting — an extended arch covering an apartment, so constructed that the stones or bricks sustain and keep each other in their places.

veneer — the skin material, a thin layer laminated to the parent body.

veranda — a porch or balcony, usually roofed and often partly enclosed, extending along the outside of a building.

vestibule — an entrance hall, ante-chamber or lobby.

wainscoting — the partial panelling of a wall, from floor to chair rail.

weatherboard — clapboard, exterior wood siding of horizontal overlapping boards.

wrought iron — iron worked with heat and shaping that both hardens and tempers, producing a linear material for grates, railings and decorations.

OUR THANKS TO:

Paul Hicks, Ron Walter, Stephan Rice Phelan, Roscoe Feild, Eleanor D. Hughes, Jeanne Crawford, Victorian Village, Inc., Nickii Elrod, Dayton Smith, May Snowden Todd, Ellen Clark Ramsay, Mrs. Karl Kaestle, Mrs. Elva Bledsoe, Mrs. Betty Reid, Mrs. Mary Winslow Chapman, Rembert Williams, Mrs. Ellen Davies Rodgers, Mrs. Alfred Feild Latting, the late Mrs. Frances Herring, Mayor Sam Wilson, Mrs. Miriam M. Wilson, George C. Hale, Harry Cloyes, Mrs. Walter D. Wills, Jr., Mrs. Reeves Hughes, Mrs. John Stivers, Mrs. James M. Russell, Mrs. Clarene Smith, Mrs. Elizabeth Parr, Ms. Mary Baker of the Landmarks Commission, Mrs. Clarence Fisher, Mrs. Henry Haizlip, and Dr. John Harkins.

Thanks, too, to those who gave interviews:

Mrs. Pat Barzizza, Jim Bennett, Ms. Priscilla Blackwell, Mayor Herman Cox, Mrs. Katherine Miller Dallum, Mrs. Paul Duke, Mrs. Mary Ann Eagle, John Sneed Ewell, Mrs. E. F. Falls, Mrs. Joe Franks, J. W. Freeman, T. Holeman Graham, Mrs. John Griffin, Mrs. James Karr Hinton, Mrs. Richard D. Holliday, Mrs. Ruth Klinke, Mrs. Charles James, the Reverend Davidson Landers, Mrs. Hunter Lane, Sr., Mrs. Freeman Marr, Mr. & Mrs. Gene T. McKenzie, Mrs. Lyman McLallen, the late Miss Louise Miller, Mrs. Jack Owen, John Patton, W. E. Patton, Mrs. Clinton Pearson, Charles Poole, Mrs. John Porter, Mrs. Demetra Patton Quinn, Mrs. Jay Rainey, Ira Samelson, Mrs. A. L. Simmons, Ms. Vickie Starr, Mrs. Carrie Sullivan, Mrs. Helen Tice, Dick Vandermark, Mr. & Mrs. Kenneth Whitlow, Mrs. Tom Williams, and Bill Fisher.

ART DIRECTION AND DESIGN:
William C. Thomas

LAYOUT AND DESIGN:
Ashley Smith
Patricia Akers
Cynthia Williams

PICTURE CREDITS

Memphis & Shelby County Public Library - inside
front liner, p. 9, p. 10, p. 23

Mississippi Valley Collection,
Memphis State University - p. 7

The Commercial Appeal - p. 46.

Memphis & Shelby County Office of Planning and
Development - inside back liner.

BIBLIOGAPHY

BOOKS

Brandau, Roberta Seawell, ed. *History of Homes and Gardens of Tennessee.* Nashville: Garden Study Club of Nashville, 1936. Reprinted by Friends of Cheekwood, 1964.

Brumbaugh, Thomas B., ed. with Strayhorn, Martha I., and Gore, Gary G. *Architecture of Middle Tennessee.* The Historic American Buildings Survey. Nashville: Vanderbilt University Press, 1974.

Burrow, Rachel Herring Kennon. *Arlington, A Short Historical Writing of the Town.* Memphis: E.H. Clarke and Brother, 1962.

Capers, Gerald M., Jr. *The Biography of a River Town.* New Orleans: Published by the author, 1966.

Chapman, M. Winslow. *I Remember Raleigh.* Memphis: Riverside Press, 1977.

Church, Annette E., and Church, Roberta. *The Robert R. Churches of Memphis.* Ann Arbor, Mich.: Edwards Brothers, 1974.

Coppock, Paul R. *Memphis Memoirs.* Memphis: Memphis State University Press, 1980.

Crawford, Charles W. *Yesterday's Memphis.* Miami: E.A. Seeman, 1976.

Davies-Rodgers, Ellen. *The Great Book, Calvary Protestant Episcopal Church, 1832-1972.* Memphis: Plantation Press, 1964.

————. *The Romance of the Episcopal Church in West Tennessee.* Memphis: Plantation Press, 1964.

Davis, James D. *The History of the City of Memphis, also The "Old Times Papers."* Memphis: Hite, Crumpton and Kelly, 1873. Reprinted by the West Tennessee Historical Society, 1972.

Durham, Walter T. *James Winchester.* Nashville: Parthenon Press, 1979.

Egerton, John. *Visions of Utopia: Nashoba, Rugby, Ruskin and the "New Communities" in Tennessee's Past.* Knoxville: University of Tennessee Press, 1977.

Goodspeed's *General History of Tennessee.* Nashville: Goodspeed Publishing Company, 1887. Reprinted by C. and R. Elder, Booksellers, 1973.

————. *History of Hamilton, Knox and Shelby Counties of Tennessee.* Nashville: Goodspeed Publishing Company, 1887. Reprinted by C. and R. Elder, Booksellers, 1974.

Harkins, John E. *Metropolis of the American Nile.* Sponsored by the West Tennessee Historical Society. Woodland Hills, California: Windsor Publications, 1982.

Hicks, Paul T. *History of First Methodist Church, Memphis, Tennessee, 1826-1900.* Memphis: Memphis Tech High School, 1980.

History of the Germantown Baptist Church. Dallas: Taylor Publishing Company, 1981.

Jemison, Peggy B. *Cherokee...History of Change.* Memphis: Metropolitan Interfaith Association, 1978.

————. *Greenlaw Rediscovered.* Memphis: Metropolitan Interfaith Association, 1979.

Keating, J.M. *History of Memphis, Tennessee.* 2 vols. Vol. 2 by O.F. Vedder. Syracuse, N.Y.: D. Mason and Company, 1888. Reprinted by Burke's Book Store.

Lee, George W. *Beale Street: Where the Blues Began.* College Park, Md.: McGrath Publishing Company, 1969.

McCorkle, Anna Leigh. *Tales of Old Whitehaven.* Jackson, Tn.: McCowat Mercer Press, 1969.

McIlwaine, Shields. *Memphis Down in Dixie.* New York: E.P. Dutton, 1948.

McKee, Margaret, and Chisenhall, Fred. *Beale Black and Blue.* Baton Rouge, La.: Louisiana State University Press, 1981.

Meriwether, Elizabeth Avery. *Recollections of Ninety-two Years, 1824-1916.* Nashville: Tennessee Historical Commission, 1958.

Miller, William D. *Mr. Crump of Memphis.* Baton Rouge, La.: Louisiana State University Press, 1964.

Myer, William E. *Indian Trails of the Southeast.* Nashville: Blue and Gray Press, 1971.

Ornelas-Struve, Carole M. and Coulter, Frederick Lee. *Memphis, 1800-1900.* Three vols. A Memphis Pink Palace Museum Book. New York: Nancy Powers and Co., 1982.

Patrick, James. *Architecture in Tennessee, 1768-1897.* Knoxville: University of Tennessee Press, 1981.

Plunkett, Kitty. *Memphis: A Pictorial History.* Norfolk, Va., 1976.

Quinn, D.A. *Heroes and Heroines of Memphis, or Reminiscences of the Yellow Fever.* Providence: E.L. Freeman and Son, 1887.

Rembert, S.S. *The Science of Life for the Wife at Home in Her Kitchen, Chamber and Parlour; or, Hygenic Philosophy.* Memphis: Boyle and Co., Publishers, 1876.

Roper, James. *The Founding of Memphis, 1818-1820.* Memphis: The Memphis Sesquicentennial, Inc., 1970.

Sigafoos, Robert A. *Cotton Row to Beale Street.* Memphis: Memphis State University Press, 1979.

Tilly, Bette B. *A Visit to Buntyn.* Memphis: Metropolitan Interfaith Association, 1979.

Trollope, Frances. *Domestic Manners of the Americans.* ed. Donald Smalley. Gloucester, Mass.: Peter Smith, 1974.

Tucker, David M. *Black Pastors and Leaders: The Memphis Clergy, 1819-1972.* Memphis: Memphis State University Press, 1975.

Wrenn, Tony P. and Mulloy, Elizabeth D. *America's Forgotten Architecture.* National Trust For Historic Preservation. New York: Pantheon, 1976.

ARTICLES

Crawford, Charles W. and McBride, Robert M. "The Magevney House, Memphis." *Tennessee Historical Quarterly.* Winter, 1969.

Griffin, John. "The Survivors: A Look At What's Left of Antebellum Memphis." *Memphis.* January, 1983.

Henderson, Debbie Kelly. "Victorian Village Blends Past Into Present." *Tennessee Conservationist,* XLII. September, 1976.

Hetlinger, Worothey. "Elmwood Cemetery." Paper submitted to Memphis Office, Federal Writers Project for Tennessee, March 4, 1936.

Holmes, Jack D.L. "Fort Ferdinand of the Bluffs, Life on the Spanish - American Frontier, 1795-1797." *West Tennessee Historical Society Publications,* XIII, 1959.

Hughes, Eleanor D. "The Fontaine House of the James Lee Memorial." *THQ.* Summer, 1968.

_____. "Landmarks of the James Lee Memorial." APTA booklet, 1977.

_____. "Two Master Architects of Early Memphis." A Souvenir of the Historic American Buildings Survey Exhibit at Brooks Memorial Art Gallery, 1971.

_____. "Victorian Village Vignettes." APTA, July 1, 1976.

Mallory, Loula G. "The Three Lives of Raleigh." *WTHSP* XIII, 1959.

Morton, Terry B. "Victorian Mansions in Memphis." *Antiques,* September, 1971.

Newcomer, Lee N. "The Battle of Memphis, 1862." *WTHSP* XIII, 1958.

Parr, Elizabeth Baker. "The History of Collierville, Tennessee." *Collierville Herald,* special edition, 1981.

Priddy, Benjamin Hugh. "Nineteenth Century Architecture in Memphis: Ten Surviving Structures." Vanderbilt University thesis, 1972.

Rayner, Juan Timoleon. "An Eyewitness Account of Forrest's Raid on Memphis." *WTHSP* XII, 1958.

Smith, Gerald P. "Chucalissa Revisited." Guide book, no date.

Sorrells, William W. "Memphis' Greatest Debate: A Study of the Development of the Public Water System." Memphis State University Master's Thesis, 1969.

Stonesifer, Roy P. "Gideon Pillow: A Study in Egotism." *THQ.* Winter, 1966.

Todd, Amie. "Old Coward Place." Paper prepared for Local History Class, Memphis State University, Fall, 1981.

Weathers, Ed. "Self-Help the Memphis Way." *Historic Preservation.* July-August, 1981.

NOTES

SOURCES

Sources consulted for each section are listed in the following order: 1-books, 2-periodicals, 3-National Register of Historic Places nomination form (NRHP), 4-pamphlets and unpublished material, 5-newspaper articles, and 6-oral interviews.

CA	*Commercial Appeal*
PS	*Press Scimitar*
THQ	*Tennessee Historical Quarterly*
WTHSP	*West Tennessee Historical Society Publications*
APTA	Association for the Preservation of Tennessee Antiquities
MIFA	Metropolitan Interfaith Association
NRHP	National Register of Historic Places Nomination Form

Court Square
1 Capers
  Harkins
  Meriwether
  Ornelas-Struve
2 Williamson, James. "The Wind Never Blew it Down." *Center City,* 10/28/7
3 NRHP
5 CA

6/17/1894	6/7/42	5/4/52	8/16/75
12/1/26	6/10/42	1/15/59	10/1/82
12/9/26	9/29/46	9/27/62	
6/24/29	6/17/47	4/25/71	
2/7/31	1/27/49	5/24/73	
9/16/38	9/22/50	8/24/74	

PS

5/2/38	11/26/51	2/9/72
3/20/42	4/27/77	8/27/80
1980 Centennial Edition		

Gayoso-Peabody District
3 NRHP
5 CA 6/11/78
         9/29/78

Downtown Churches
1 Hicks
  Ornelas-Struve
  Tucker
2 Hughes, Eleanor D., "Two Master Architects of Early Memphis," A Souvenir of the HABS Exhibit at Brooks Memorial Art Gallery, 1971.
  LaBadie, Donald, "Architecture as a Reflection of Alteration of Society," *CA,* 1/27/80.
  Priddy, Benjamin H., "Nineteenth Century Architecture in Memphis: Ten Surviving Structures." Vanderbilt University thesis, 1972.
3 NRHP

4 "Calvary Church in Memphis" brochure
  "First Presbyterian Church," two brochures
  "The Heritage of St. Peter's," brochure
  "Trinity Lutheran Church, 1855-1980" brochure
5 CA

1/1/40	3/12/67
10/26/64	10/31/70
2/12/67	3/11/71
3/4/67	5/22/76

PS

3/1/35	8/29/39
6/20/38	10/27/73
9/6/38	4/26/74
9/7/38	10/11/80

Cotton Row
1 Capers
  Harkins
  McIlwaine
2 Bennett, Ann K., "Designation Report, Cotton Row Historic District," Memphis Landmarks Commission, 1977.

Beale Street
1 Lee
  McKee & Chisenhall
  Sigafoos
4 "Beale Street, U.S.A." February, 1954.
  "The Blue Light District of Beale Street, Memphis, Tennessee," An Architectural and Historical Survey for the Memphis Housing Authority, n.d.
5 Coppock, Paul. "Drinks, Rooms, Justice at Gallina's Exchange," *CA,* 12/28/75.
  Donahue, Michael, "Image of Zesty Life on Beale Street Paves 84-Year-Old's Memory," *PS,* 2/21/81.
  Smith, Whitney, "Uncovering the History of Beale Street," *CA,* 2/20/83.
  "I Remember Beale Street," A Non-Fiction Television Program on PBS.

Hunt-Phelan House
1 Brandau
  Meriwether
  Ornelas-Struve
3 NRHP
4 Survey and Presentation Plan of Memphis Landmarks Commission, September, 1980.
5 CA

8/7/49	7/26/71
7/19/62	12/29/73

PS 10/4/36
6 Untaped interview with Elder Blair T. Hunt by Selma Lewis and Marjean Kremer for MIFA, Dec. 15, 1977.
  Interviews with Stephen Rice Phelan, 1983.

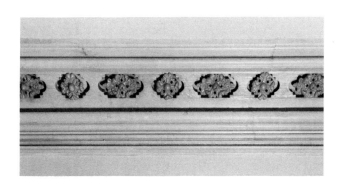

Magevney House
1 Keating
  Ornelas-Struve
2 Crawford, Charles, and McBride, Robert H., "The Magevney House, Memphis," *THQ*, Winter, 1969.
  Johnson, Jill, "Historic Dresser Home to Stay," *PS*, 9/17/82.
3 NRHP
6 Interview with Susan Olsen, curator, by Mary Davis, 9/18/82.

Adams Avenue
3 NRHP
4 Cox, W.P., F.A.I.A., "Architectural Analysis of the First James Lee House," June 15, 1977.
  Gaskill, William H., NRHP, August 7, 1974.
  Hughes, Eleanor D., "The First James Lee House," Unpublished manuscript, June 10, 1977.
  Victorian Village Walking Tour Guide.
  Elmwood Cemetery Records, 1874.
5 *United Labor Journal*, October 25, 1900.
  Memphis Evening Scimitar Art Supplement, no date.
  CA   1/10/51
6 Interviews with Eleanor D. Hughes, Roscoe A. Feild and Mrs. E.F. Falls (granddaughter of Thomas R. Boyle).

Victorian Village
1 Harkins
  Ornelas-Struve
2 Henderson, Debbie Kelly, "Victorian Village Blends Past Into Present," *Tennessee Conservationist*, Vol. XLII, September, 1976.
  Hughes, Eleanor D., "Two Master Architects of Early Memphis," A Souvenir of the HABS Exhibit at Brooks Memorial Art Gallery, 1971.
  Hughes, Eleanor D., "Victorian Vignettes," 7/1/76.
  Hughes, Eleanor D., "Landmarks of the James Lee Memorial." APTA brochure, 1977.
  Hughes, Eleanor D., "The Fontaine House of the James Lee Memorial," *THQ*, Summer, 1968.
  Morton, Terry B., "Victorian Mansions in Memphis," *Antiques*, September, 1971.
  Stonesifer, Roy P., "Gideon Pillow: A Study in Egotism," *THQ*. Winter, 1966.
  "Memphis Victorian Village Offers Look at the Past," *Preservation News*, September, 1974.
  "Old Memphis Homes on Tour," *Tennessee Historical Places*, 1961.
3 NRHP
4 APTA Heritage Tour, May 6-7, 1967.
  "APTA Preserves the Fontaine House and the James Lee Memorial" brochure.

"In the Days of Miss Daisy, 100 Years of a Family, A House, A City," The Mallory-Neely House, DAR-SAR-CAR, 1974.
Mrs. Helen Tice, new hostess information, Mallory-Neely House, 1983.

5	*CA*	2/24/57	8/12/69	8/8/73
		8/16/66	7/14/72	7/16/76
	PS	12/7/62	7/5/66	2/24/82
		7/31/64	1/5/73	

Lowenstein House
1 Keating, Vol. II.
3 NRHP
5 *PS*   10/23/53
       10/24/54
6 Interview with Ira Samelson.

Bradford-Maydwell House
3 NRHP
5 *CA*   6/9/81
  PS   3/17/82

Patton House
3 NRHP
4 Four Flames Restaurant Pamphlet.
5 *CA*   3/30/65
       3/31/65
  PS   3/30/65
       3/31/65
       8/1/79
6 Interviews with W.E. Patton, Jr., John Patton and Demetra Patton Quinn by Susan Patton Robinson, March, 1983.

Vance-Pontotoc District
3 NRHP
5 *CA*   8/3/81
       2/8/38
       3/11/38
  PS   3/20/31
       9/11/59
       4/7/82

Old Coward Place
4 Smith, Janet Stuart. Menu notes from Justine's.
  Todd, Amie, "Old Coward Place," Paper prepared for Local History Class, Memphis State University, Fall, 1981.
5 Cunter, James, "Old Home Being Renovated to House Famous Restaurant," *CA*, 2/23/58.
  Davis, Anna Byrd, "Restaurants in Historic Houses Offer Diners Trip Back in Time," *PS*, 11/7/58.
  Raymond, Mary, "Stately Home Restored to Earliest Grandeur," *PS*, 11/7/58.

Talley, Robert, "The Old Coward Place," *CA*, 5/4/41.
6   Interview with Dayton Smith.

Elmwood Cemetery
4   Hetlinger, Worothey, "Elmwood Cemetery," Paper submitted to Memphis Office, Federal Writers Project, 3/4/36.
Prices and Charges of Elmwood Cemetery, 1910.
Rules and Regulations of Elmwood Cemetery, 1928.
Rules and Regulations of Elmwood Cemetery, 1954.
Elmwood: Charter, Rules, Regulations and By-laws, 1978.
"Touring Historic Elmwood Cemetery," brochure, 1978.

5   *CA*   6/20/49   6/10/78   9/13/81
8/31/52   7/15/78   3/13/81
5/26/52   7/27/78   8/25/82
5/2/55   5/21/79
PS   6/2/53   10/19/74

Greenlaw
1   Capers
Crawford
Harkins
Jemison
Sigafoos
2   Griffin, John, "The Survivors: A Look At What's Left of Antebellum Memphis," *Memphis*, January, 1983.
Sorrells, William M., "Memphis' Greatest Debate: A Study of the Development of the Public Water System," MSU Master's Thesis, 1969.
Weathers, Ed, "Self-Help the Memphis Way," *Historic Preservation*, July-August, 1981.
4   "History of Memphis Water," Memphis Light, Gas and Water Division, no date.
"Nineteenth Century Churches of Downtown Memphis," APTA, 1974.
"Porter Leath Children's Center History," no date.
"Water Works," *United Labor Journal*, 1910.
3   NRHP
5   *CA*   7/19/76
PS   7/10/79
12/15/82
6   Notes of a conversation with Mrs. Catherine L. Compton by Eleanor McKay and Lou Gruenberg, November 1, 1977, Mississippi Valley Collection, MSU.

Rozelle House
4   Elmwood Cemetery files, 1873.
Hughes, Eleanor D., "Notes to Heritage Tour," 1961.
5   *PS*   3/21/61   1/13/81
6   Interview with Mrs. Richard D. Holliday by Ginny Strubing, 1982.

Rayner House
2   Poole, Charles E., "The Eli Rayner House." speech delivered at meeting of the Southwestern History Club, February 20, 1949.
Rayner, Juan Timoleon, "An Eyewitness Account of Forrest's Raid on Memphis," *WTHSP*, XII, 1958.
3   NRHP
6   Interviews with Nickii Elrod and Eleanor D. Hughes by Becky Deupree, 1982.

Annesdale and Ashlar Hall
1   Brandau
2   Morton, Terry B., "Victorian Mansions of Memphis," *Antiques*, September, 1971.
3   NRHP
4   "Midtown," brochure published by First Tennessee Bank, no date.
History of the Annesdale-Snowden Association.
5   *CA*   10/12/42   2/29/57
10/13/42   2/9/57
PS   3/18/31
10/13/42
7/29/64
6   Interview with May Snowden Todd by Ainslie Todd, 1982.

Ramsay House
1   Brandau
Tilly
4   Scrapbook of Ellen Ramsay Clark.
5   *CA*   5/20/56
PS   2/25/65

Maxwellton
1   Tilly
3   NRHP
6   Interview with John Sneed Ewell by Ginny Strubing, 1982.

Elam Homestead
1   Jemison
3   NRHP
5   Clemens, Ida, "Essence of Pioneer Ways Throws it Aura Over Quaint Memphis Home," *CA*, 5/23/37.
Pittman, Kay, "165-Year-Old Home Goes on Market," *PS*, 3/29/63.

Richards House
4   Biography of Newton C. Richards in *Tennessee, The Volunteer State, 1796-1923*, Vol. III, Published by S.J. Clarke, 1923.
5   Tamke, Beth J., "Victorian Values," *CA*, 1/23/83.
6   Interview with Vickie Starr by Ginny Strubing, 1983.

Captain Harris House
3 NRHP
5 *CA* 1/10/80

Tennessee Brewery
1 Plunkett
2 Rowland, Marilyn and Geoghan, Brenda, "Convertible Assets: The Tennessee Brewery and Other Possibilities," *City of Memphis*, June, 1977.
5 *CA* 6/1/13   5/20/32   12/20/56
         2/27/17   5/17/36
         5/21/32   2/28/42
6 Interview with Rona Newburger, 1982.

Marine Hospital
3 NRHP

Raleigh
1 Capers
   Chapman
   Harkins
2 Mallory, Loula G., "The Three Lives of Raleigh," *WTHSP*, XIII, 1959.
3 NRHP
4 Coppock, Paul, "Raleigh Springs," in pamphlet printed by Commerce Title Company, 1961.
6 Interviews with Mrs. Mary Chapman by Ginny Strubing, 1982-83, Mrs. Lyman McLallen and T. Holeman Graham by Ginny Strubing, 1983. Interview with Mrs. Charles James by Penny Dart, May, 1981.

Seven Hills Plantation
1 Rembert
5 "Old South Remembered at Seven Hills Plantation," *Millington Star*, February 11, 1982.
   Porteous, Clark, "Early Shelbian's Shiloh Journey Tough and Sad," *PS*, 7/14/67.
6 Interviews with Rembert Williams by Ainslie Todd and Linda Smith, 1982, and by Ginny Strubing, 1983.

Ellendale - Cedar Hall
4 APTA Heritage House Town and Country Tour notes, 1973.
   Cooper, Mrs. H. W., "Ellendale Cemetery and Historical Notes," 1947.
   "Be Independent For Life," booklet published by Ellendale Land and Improvement Company, no date.
5 *CA* 4/27/73
         10/22/66
   PS 9/21/66

Brunswick
3 NRHP
4 Printed folder from Davies Manor, 1981.

5 *CA* 10/29/46
         7/25/65
         5/27/79
   PS 8/7/44
         3/6/51
6 Interviews with Ellen Davies Rodgers and Mrs. John Griffin, 1983, by Ginny Strubing.

Bartlett
1 Goodspeed
   Keating
4 Coppock, Paul, "Shelby's Five Towns," pamphlet published by Commerce Title Company, 1961.
   "The History of Bartlett," pamphlet and map, 1981.
   Biographical notes on Nicholas Blackwell from Bartlett High School.
   Biographical notes on Nicholas Gotten from *Confederate Military History*, Vol. VIII, Tennessee, (Atlanta: Confederate Publishing Company, 1899).
5 *CA* 3/30/73
   PS 6/9/67
6 Interviews with Mrs. Elva Bledsoe, Mrs. Ruth Klinke, Mrs. Clinton Pearson, Mr. J.W. Freeman, Mrs. Katherine Miller Dallum, Miss Louise Miller, Mr. and Mrs. Gene T. McKenzie, Mrs. Betty Reid, Mr. Dick Vandemark, Mrs. Mary Ann Eagle, and Mrs. Freeman Marr.

Cordova
4 Brough, Augusta Hooper, "History of Cordova," unpublished manuscript, 1952.
   Latting, Mrs. Alfred Feild, "Mt. Airy History," 1983.
   "History of Cordova Presbyterian Church," no date.
5 *CA* 4/29/77
   PS 1/17/83.

Arlington
1 Burrow
   Goodspeed
3 NRHP
4 Wilson, Miriam M., Remarks at Shelby County Historical Commission Banquet, November 2, 1981
6 Interviews with Mr. Sam T. Wilson by Becky Deupree and Nancy Chase, 1982, and Mrs. Frances Herring by Ginny Strubing and Helen Hays, 1983.

Germantown
1 Egerton
   Goodspeed
   Keating
4 Coppock, Paul, "Shelby's Five Towns," pamphlet published by Commerce Title Company, 1961.
   History of the Germantown Baptist Church (Dallas: Taylor Publishing Company, 1981).

Hughes, Betty Powell, "Germantown Presbyterian Church," unpublished manuscript, 1983.

Hughes, Betty Powell, "Richwood," unpublished manuscript, 1983.

Wills, Dorothy Kirby, "Woodlawn," unpublished manuscript, 1983.

5   Germantown DAR, "How It Began," *Germantown News*, 1/7/71.

Germantown Independent
     5/14/75
     5/7/75

Germantown News
     10/20/75   6/23/77
     5/7/75   8/24/78
     11/18/76

CA   3/13/38
     1/1/40
     5/2/48

PS   6/19/80

6   Interviews with Mr. Harry Cloyes, Mrs. Reeves Hughes, Mrs. Virginia Stivers, Mrs. Carrie Sullivan, Mrs. Tom Williams, Mrs. Walter D. Wills, Jr., Mr. and Mrs. Kenneth Whitlow, Mrs. Eleanor Woodward.

Mosby-Bennett House

3   NRHP
6   Interview with Mrs. Hunter Lane, Sr.

Collierville

1   Goodspeed
    Harkins
    Grant, U.S. *Personal Memoirs of U.S. Grant.* 2 vol. N.Y.: Charles L. Webster, 1885. Vol. I, pp. 387-389.
    Sherman, William T. *Memoirs.* 2 vol. N.Y.: D. Appleton and Co., 1913. Vol. I, pp. 378-381.
    Contemporary Club. *Old Homes, Old Churches, Old Places, Collierville.*

4   Material from the Files of Mrs. James M. Russell.
    Holden, Mrs. Kate, "A Short Sketch of the History of St. Andrew's Church," June, 1912.
    "A History of St. Andrew's Episcopal Church, Collierville, Tennessee, and How the Work Started," 1955.
    Coppock, Paul, "Shelby's Five Towns," 1961.

5   Parr, Elizabeth Baker, "The History of Collierville, Tennessee," 1949. In Special Edition of the *Collierville Herald*, 1981.
    CA   7/25/76
         2/18/57
         4/15/70
    PA   4/8/48
         6/1/67
         4/14/72
         10/22/76
         3/19/81
         12/27/82

6   Interviews with Mrs. James Russell, Mrs. Elizabeth Parr, Mrs. Paul Duke, Mayor Herman Cox, Mrs. Jack Owen by Becky Deupree and Snow Morgan. Interview with Mrs. John Porter by Marietta Haaga.

Whitehaven

1   McCorkle
4   1850 Shelby County Census.
    1821-1870 General Index of Deeds.
    1819-1950 Shelby County Marriage Records.
5   *CA*   1/3/62
6   Interviews with George C. Hale and Mrs. Harris Bailey, 1983.
    Information from members of the Hilderbrand family, Mrs. Karl Kaestle, Maurine Hilderbrand Howlett and John Edward Elam.

INDEX

A

Abington, J.B. 151, 163
Adams Avenue 10, 47-54
Adams, Fort 8, 14
Adams, President John 108
"Akron Plan" 34, 79
Allen, Betsy Ecklin 128
Allen, Jim 128
Allen, Thomas 128
Alston, Rev. Philip 28
Anderson, Mr. 142
Anderson, Mrs. Mildred 88
Annesdale 10, 90-93
Annesdale-Snowden Historic District 90-93
Arlington 14, 127, 132-135
Armour, Olsey Bail 163
Arnold, Herman Frank 87
Art Academy 63, 65-66
Artesian Water Company 82
Ashlar Hall 94
Association for the Preservation of Tennessee Antiquities
  (APTA) 64-66
Assumption, Fort 8, 14

B

Babb, Benjamin 56
Baldwin, Matthias Harvey 42, 51, 54, 63, 66
Bankhead, Tallulah 71
Bartlett 13, 14, 116-121, 127
Bartlett, Major Gabriel 116
Beale Street 13, 39-46
Beale Street Baptist Church 38, 42-43
Beane, Samuel Jackson 133
Bejach, L.D. 76
Bejach, Samuel 76
Bennett, George H. 148
Bethel, Lemuel Hall 140
Bettis, Tillman 95
Beurer, James 142
Beyer, Pastor John 33
Bickford, W.A. 28
Bienville, Sieur de (Jean Baptiste LeMoyne) 8, 14
Big Creek 9
Biggs, J.T. 161
Blackwell, George 118
Blackwell House, Bartlett 118
Blackwell, John 118
Blackwell, Nicholas 118-119
Blackwell, Virginia Ward 118
Bohlen-Huse Ice Company 82
Bond, John 125
Bond, Margaret Ann (Peggy) 125

Bond, Mary Lucy Tate 125
Bond, Nicholas Pirtle 125
Bond, Dr. Samuel 125
Bond, Washington 125
Bond's Station (Ellendale) 125-127
Bone, Dr. G.P. 134
Bone House, Arlington 134-135
Booth, Mrs. 143
Boyle, Margaret Owen 52
Boyle, Thomas Raymond 52
Bradford-Maydwell House 75
Bradford, W.C. 75
Brinkley, Robert C. 91
Britton, William Johnstone 25
Brooks, Agnes Nelson Dandridge 144
Brooks, Joseph 144
Brooks, Patsy 144
Brooks, S.H. 56
Brooks, Wilks 137, 140, 144
Brunswick 122-124, 127
Bryan, Charles 116
Buerer, Jacob 83
Buerer, Rosina Burkle 83
Buntyn, Geraldus 100
Buntyn, Dr. G.O. 100
Buntyn-Ramsay House 100-101
Buntyn's Station 100, 102
Burkle House 83
Burkle, Jacob 83
Burkle, Maria Rebecca Vorwerk 83

C

Callis, A.T. 143
Callis, Minor 143
Calvary Episcopal Church 27-29, 47
Captain Harris House 103
Carr, Anderson 95
Carroll, Major-General William 88
Cartwright, Monroe 153
Cedar Hall, Ellendale 10, 125-127
Chalmers, General James R. 151
Chapman, E. Winslow 114
Chapman, Mary Winslow 114
Chickasaw Gardens 100
Church, Robert Sr. 40, 87
Church's Auditorium 40
Clayborn, Bishop John Henry 38
Clayborn Temple (Second Presbyterian Church) 27, 38
Cleveland, President Grover 18, 64
Clouston, Joe 40
Coleman, James M. 112
Collier, Jesse R. 150

Collierville 11-12, 14, 150-165
Collierville Presbyterian Church 151, 162-163
Continental Bank (D.T. Porter Building) 18-19
Cook, Annie 87
Cook, James B. 11, 17, 27-28, 32-33
Cordova 128-131, 146
Cornelius, Dr. J.M.M. 143
Co-She-Co 146
Cotton Row 22-25
Court Square 11, 16-21, 113
Coward, Ida Carroll 88
Coward Place (Justine's) 88-89
Coward, Samuel 88
Craine, William 157
Crane, William 11
Cranfield, William 157
Crenshaw, Ellen Feild 130
Crenshaw, Thomas C. 130
Crump, E.H. 80, 86, 106
Cruse, Samuel Ridgely 71

D

DAR-SAR-CAR (Daughters of the American Revolution,
  Sons of the American Revolution, Children of the
  American Revolution) 59
Dalton, Kit 87
Davidson, Reverend Thomas 34
Davies, Frances Anna Vaughan 122
Davies, James Baxter 122
Davies, Logan Early 122
Davies Manor, Brunswick 10, 122-123
Davies, William E. 122
Davies, Zacariah 122
Davis, Charles R. 157
Davis, Charles Robert 157
Davis, Jefferson 11, 44, 46, 60, 86, 88
Davis-Porter House, Collierville 156-157
Davis, Laura Theresa Taylor 157
DeLoach House, Collierville 152-153
DeLoach, Huldah Dean 152
DeLoach, Josiah 152-153
DeLoach, Olivia Hill 152
DeLoach, William 152
DeSoto, Hernando 7, 14
Driver, Col. Eli Moore 44
Driver, Julia 44
DuBois, W.E.B. 40
Duke, W. 112
Dwyer, John 132

E

Eads (Leakeville) 154

Ecklin House (Holly Hills), Cordova 10, 116, 128-129
Ecklin, Joshua 128
Ecklin, Lucinda Edwards 129
Ecklin, Robert 116, 128, 130
Edmondson, Thurman 139
Edwards, Ace 116, 129
Egypt, Tennessee 9
Elam, Edward Simpson 98, 167
Elam Homestead 10, 98-99
Elam, John Simpson 98
Elam, Sarah 98
Elder, James 71
Ellendale 125-127
Ellet, Judge H.T. 64
Elmwood Cemetery 12, 86-87, 144
Estival Park 105
Eudora Baptist Church 100
Evans, Rev. Richard R. 139
Ewell, John Sneed 102

F

Farley, J. Boyce 158
Farley, Nancy Fleming 158
Faulkner, William C. 103
Feild, Charles Granison 130
Feild, Emily Augusta Ecklin 130
Feild, Roscoe 130
First Baptist Beale Street 38, 42-43
First Baptist Church, Memphis 100
First Methodist Church 34-35
First Presbyterian Church 27, 36-37
Fleming, Mrs. A.B. Sullivan 158
Fleming, Eliza Moseley 158
Fleming, Fannie Gooch 158
Fleming, John 158
Fleming Place, Collierville 158-159
Fleming, Samuel 158
Fletcher, Martha Ellen Leake 154
Fletcher, Dr. Maurice 154
Fontaine House 13, 62-64
Fontaine, Noland 63, 68
Fontaine, Virginia 63
Ford, Ford Maddox 114
Forrest, Mattie Patton 76
Forrest, General Nathan Bedford 11, 44-45, 76, 86, 96, 113,
  121, 151
Fort Pickering 10, 14
Fowlkes, Austin 52
Fowlkes-Boyle House 52-53
Fowlkes, Sterling 52
Frank, Monroe 153
Freedman's Bureau 12, 40

Freeman, James 112
Frick, G.W. 142
Furstenheim, Louisa 142

G
Galloway, Robert M. 142
Gamble, Lottie Quackenbush 50
Gayoso Hotel 10, 26, 39, 88
Gayoso, Don Manuel 8
Gayoso-Peabody Historic District 26
Germantown 12, 14, 136-147
Germantown Baptist Church 137, 139, 140, 144
Germantown Presbyterian Church 137, 138-139
Gingerbread Playhouse and Nineteenth Century Dollhouse 65
Glendale 116-117
Goodwin, William Washington 113-114
Goodwinslow 113-114
Gotten, David Henry 121
Gotten, Julia Coleman 121
Gotten House, Bartlett 121
Gotten, Leona 121
Gotten, Maggie Amelia 121
Gotten, Nicholas 121
Gotten, Peter Monroe 121
Gould, Edwin 79
Goyer, Charles Wesley 65-66, 70, 79
Goyer, Charlotte Harsson 66
Goyer, Laura Harsson 66
Goyer-Lee House 66-67
Graham, Albert 115
Graham House, Raleigh 115
Graham, Joseph 112, 115
Grant, General Ulysses S. 11, 18, 36, 40, 44-45, 148, 152-153
Graves, Richard 82
Gray, John M. 142
Gray, Rev. W.C. 164
Green, Bishop 164
Green Gables, Arlington 133-134
Greenlaw 10, 13-14, 77ff
Greenlaw, J. Oliver 10, 77
Greenlaw, William Borden 10, 77
Griffin House, Brunswick 124
Griffin, John 124
Grosvenor, Hosea Merrill 88
Grotto of Our Lady of Lourdes 32, 48
Guion, Isaac 8
Guthrie, Sylva D'Arusmont 136

H
Hadden, David Park 13, 86

Hale, George R. 166
Hale House, Whitehaven 166
Hall, Richard Robert Redford 148
Hall, William Lawrence 148
Halley, Francis 150
Halliburton, Richard 114
Hamilton, Kate Magevney 32, 48-49
Hamilton, General T.C. 45
Hamner family 158
Handwerker, J.V. 65
Handy Park 39
Handy, W.C. 39-42
Harris, Captain 103
Harris, Dr. George W.D. 79
Harris, Governor Isham Green 86, 102
Harris Memorial Methodist Church 79
Harsson, William 60, 66
Hays, Robert Butler 132
Hays, Samuel Jackson 132
Haysville (Arlington) 132
Hearn, Lafcadio 22
Henning, James 63
Herbers, Christina Mette 54
Herbers, George 54
Herron House, Arlington 134-135
Hilderbrand, Judge Abraham 167
Hilderbrand, Benjamin 166
Hilderbrand, Daniel 166
Hilderbrand, Emma Elam 98, 167
Hilderbrand, Susan Robertson 167
Hill, Duncan 152
Hill, Duncan Jr. 152
Hill, Harry 152-153
Hill, Jerome 152
Hill, Napolean 10, 152
Hodges, Louisa Rayner 96
Hodges, Dr. W.R. 96
Holden, Anna 164
Holly Hills Country Club (Ecklin House) 10, 116, 128
Hooper, J.S. 151
Horsfall, Lord Thomas Marsh 127
Howard Association 12, 96
Hughes, Mabel Williams 134
Humphreys, Mary Eudora Stratton 161, 163
Humphreys, Turner 161, 163
Hunt, Elder Blair T. 46, 87
Hunt-Phelan House 11, 40, 44-46
Hunt, Sarah Elizabeth Driver 44
Hunt, Colonel William Richardson 44

I
Independent Order of Odd Fellows 78

Irby, Harrison 151, 154
Irving Block 11, 17, 121

J
Jackson, Andrew 8-9, 14, 16, 125, 132, 136
Jefferson Avenue Townhouses 71
Jefferson, President Thomas 136
Jeffreys, Mr. 139
Johnson, General Albert Sidney 130
Johnston, Elizabeth Coward 88
Johnston, Richard O. 88
Joliet, Louis 7, 14
Jones, Edward Culliatt 18, 27, 36, 38, 42, 51, 54, 63, 66, 71, 78
Jones, Governor James C. "Lean Jimmy" 86
Joy, Levi 102
Justine's (Coward Place) 88-89

K
Karsh, Blanche Hamilton 48-49
Keely, Patrick C. 30
Kees and Long 38
Keys, Reverend Scott 42
Kimble, J. 98
Kindred, E.G. 161
Kirtland, Isaac B. 56
Koen, John W. 50
Ku Klux Klan 12, 40

L
Lafayette, Marquis de 136
LaSalle 7, 14, 136
Latham, J.G. 82
Lawrence, Uncle Harry 34
Lawrence, William 9, 14, 16
Leake, Elgin K. 152
Leake House, Collierville 154-155
Leake, Millard Fillmore 154
Leake, Richard 154
Leake, Samuel 154
Leake, Tingnal H. 154
Leake, Dr. Virginius 151, 154
Leakeville (Eads) 154
Leath, Mrs. Sarah 78
Lee, First James House 50-51
Lee-Fontaine Carriage House 65
Lee, James Jr. 50, 66
Lee, James Sr. 50
Lee, Rosa 63, 65-66
LeMoyne, Jean Baptiste (Sieur de Bienville) 8
Lilly, Helen M. 120
Lindsay, Vachel 114

Love, George Collins 80-81
Love House 80-81
Love, Mary 80
Love, Octavia 80
Lowenstein, Babette Wolff 72
Lowenstein, Elias 72ff
Lowenstein House 72-74
Lucken, Anthony 137

M
McAleer, Father Michael 30
McClung, Charles 143
McCombs, J.M. 70
McGehee, Edward 158
McIlwaine, Sheilds 22, 28
McIntyre, Ella Goyer 70
McIntyre, Florence 66, 70
McIntyre, Peter 70
McKeon, William 48
McLemore, John C. 10
McNutt, Reverend A.G. 139
Maddux, Dr. Snowden Craven 124
Magevney, Eugene 10, 14, 16, 32, 48-49
Magevney House 10, 47-49
Magevney, Mary 48-49
Magevney, Mary Smyth 48-49
Mah-Ti-A-Cha 146
Mallory, Barton Lee 56
Mallory, Frances Neely, "Miss Daisy" 56ff
Mallory-Neely House 56-59
Malone, James H. 16
Mangum, Joseph 164
Mangum, Mary Louise 164
Manning, John 48
Mansfield, Dr. Samuel 91
Marine Hospital 108
Marley House, Arlington 133-134
Marley's Crossing 150
Marquette, Jacques 7, 14
Marysville (Cordova) 11, 128
Massey, Benjamin 60
Massey House 60-61
Massey, Tennessee (Germantown) 144
Maxwelton 102
Maydwell, James 60, 66, 75
Maydwell, Sophia Harsson 60, 66
Meagher, Paddy 8
Memphis Art Association Free School 66, 70
Memphis and Charleston Railroad 10, 14, 39, 95-96, 100, 137, 144, 150
Memphis Cotton Exchange 15, 23, 105
Memphis Country Club 100

Memphis Little Theater 65
Memphis Merchants Exchange 23
Mercer, J.A. 134
Meriwether, Elizabeth Avery 17, 45, 72
Mette, Herman Henry 54
Mette House 54
Miller, Benjamin Robinson 118
Miller, Louise 118
Miller, Willie Blackwell 118
Moody, Thommas L. 137
Moon, Ginny 87
Morning Sun 11, 128, 130, 154
Mosby-Bennett House 148-149
Mosby, Joseph 148
Mosby, Samuel 148
Mt. Airy 130-131

N
Nashoba 9, 14, 136-137
National Ornamental Iron Museum 108
Neely, James Columbus 56
Neely, Moses 139
New Harmony, Indiana 9
New Hope Baptist Church 137, 140
New Prospect Baptist Church 42
Nick-e-Yea 158
Nolley House, Collierville 163
Nuns of St. Mary's 12, 87

O
Oak Grove (Collierville) 50
Orgill, Edmund 127
Overton, John 8-9, 14, 16, 91, 112
Owen, Reverend Francis 34
Owen, Robert 9
Park, Mayor John 11
Parrish, Joel 17
Patrick, Sabrina Ecklin 128
Patrick, William 128
Patton, Helen Coulter 76
Patton House 76
Patton, Mollie Terry 76
Patton, Thomas Newton 76
Pea Ridge (Germantown) 137, 144
Peabody, George 91
Peabody Hotel 26
Person, William 87
Peters, Thomas Hill 152
Phelan, William Richardson Hunt 46
Pickering, Timothy 8
Pierce, Bishop 164
Pike, Zebulon 8

Pillow, General Gideon Johnson 70
Pillow-McIntyre House 10, 70
Pinch 10
Pittman, Henry Munger 133
Polk, President James K. 70, 86
Polk, General Leonidas 44
Porter, Dr. D.T. 13, 18-19, 27, 78, 86, 142
Porter, D.T. Building 18-19
Porter-Leath Children's Center 78-79
Pulliam, Elijah 116
Pulliam, Pamela Nelson Massey 116

Q
Quintard, Bishop 164

R
Raleigh 8, 14, 16, 80, 112-116
Ralston, John 115
Ramsay, Mrs. Henry Ashton 101
Ramsay, Jack W. 101
Ramsey, John 8, 14, 88
Ramsey, Richard 151
Randolph 9, 112
Ransom, John Crowe 114
Rawlings, Isaac 8, 167
Rayner, Eli 96
Rayner, Eli Jr. 96
Rayner House 96-97
Rayner, Juan Timoleon 96
Rayner, May Jones 96
Rembert, Andrew 110
Rembert, Ann Duncan 110
Rembert, Henry 110
Rembert, Sam 110
Rembert, Samuel Stokes 110-111
Rhodes, Mary B. 142
Rice, John 8, 14, 144
Richards House 104-105
Richards, Louise Mather 105
Richards, Newton Copeland 105
Richardson, C.G. 70
Richmond, Dr. Leonidas Polk 146
Richwood, Germantown 146-147
Ridgeway (Germantown) 144
Riggs, Daniel M. 146
Rodgers, Ellen Davies 122
Roosevelt, President Theodore 20, 40, 42
Royster, Joel 122
Rozelle, Blackmon 95
Rozelle, C.W. 95
Rozelle House 95
Rozelle, Mary 95

Rozelle, Solomon 95
Rutland, Euzelia Buntyn 101
Rutland, George W. 101

S
St. Andrew's Episcopal Church, Collierville 152, 164-165
St. John's Episcopal Church 102
St. Mary's Roman Catholic Church 11, 27, 32, 48
St. Peter's Roman Catholic Church 30-31, 47-48
Salem Presbyterian Church 158, 162
Samelson, Celia Lowenstein 74
San Fernando de las Barrancas 7-8, 14
Sander, Dr. Enno 112
Sanderlin, Wilson 112
Sanderlin's Bluff 9, 16, 112
Saunders, Clarence 120
Schorr, Jacob 106
Schorr, John 106
Schorr, John Jr. 106
Scott, Susan Elder 71
Scott, William I. 71
Second Presbyterian Church (Clayborn Temple) 27, 38
Seven Hills Plantation 110-111
Sharpe, Laura Elam 98
Shelby, Isaac 8-9
Shelton, Edward W. 134
Shelton House, Arlington 133-134
She-Mi-O-Kay 157
Shepherd-Arthur House, Germantown 141
Shepherd, Colonel G.P. 137
Shepherd, Nicey B. 142
Sherman, General William Tecumseh 11, 28, 151
Siedakum, F. 143
Sledge, William D. 71
Smith-McKenzie House, Bartlett 119
Sneed, Judge John Louis Taylor 102
Snowden, Annie Overton Brinkley 91ff
Snowden, John Bayard 93
Snowden, Robert Bogardus 91ff
Snowden, Robert Brinkley 93-94
Snowden, Roberta Galloway 93
Snyder, Jacob 34
Sodom 10, 39
Sousa, John Philip 64
South Memphis 10, 14, 39
Spickernagle, Mayor William 10, 86
Spottswood, E.A. 102
Stratton, Dr. A.S. 158, 161, 163
Stratton-Owen House, Collierville 160-161
Stratton, Mary Elizabeth Chamberlain 161
Sullivan House, Germantown 143
Swazey, Nelson 16

T
Tall Cedar Cottage, Arlington 132, 134
Tapp's Hole (Raleigh) 112
Tate, Allen 114
Tate, Jesse Minor 44, 125
Taxing District 13, 18, 82
Taylor, Andrew 157
Taylor House 68-69
Taylor, Mollie Fontaine 68
Taylor, Dr. William Wood 68
Taylor, President Zachary 8, 157
Tennessee Brewery 106-107
Tennessee Club 20-21
Terrell, Edward 20
Thompson, Florida C. 143
Titus, James 143
Todd, May Snowden 93
Todd, Thomas Hardy Jr. 93
Ton Tubby 167
Toof House 51
Toof, John S. 51
Toof, S.C. 142
Topp, Robertson 10, 39
Trezevant, J.T. 39
Trimble, Frank 103
Trinity Lutheran Church 27, 33
Turley, Irene Rayner 96
Turley, Senator Thomas Battle 96
Turner, Mr. 143

U
Union Depot (Bartlett) 116-121

V
Van Buren, President Martin 167
Vance-Pontotoc Historic District 84
Victorian Village Historic District 47, 55-71

W
Walsh, John 65
Waring Sewers 13, 82
Warren, Robert Penn 114
Washington, Booker T. 40
Waters, O.E. 46
Wells, Ida B. 42
Western Sanitary Commission 46
White, Col. Francis M. 166
White, Rev. George 164
Whitehaven 166-167
Whitlow House, Germantown 143
Wigfall, Senator 151
Will-Hugh, Arlington 132, 133-134

Williams, Crittenden 134
Williams House, Germantown 142
Williams, Mary 128
Williams, Rembert 110
Willis, Joseph 50
Wilson, Uncle Nathan 46
Wilson, Mayor Sam 133
Wilson's General Store, Arlington 133
Winchester, Gen. James 8, 9, 16, 150
Winchester, Marcus 9, 14, 16
Winslow, Eveleth 114
Winslow, Anne Goodwin 114
Winston, Dorothea Spottswood Henry 87
Woodlawn 144-145
Woodruff, Amos 63
Wooldridge, Mollie Woodruff 63
Wright, Camilla 136
Wright Carriage House 71
Wright, Eldridge 71
Wright, Frances (Fanny) 9, 14, 136-137
Wright, Gen. Luke E. 71
Wright, Rev. Thomas 28
Wyatt, George 39, 44
Wythe Depot (Arlington) 11, 127, 132
Yates, Foster 120
Yates-Marr House, Bartlett 120
Yates, Mattie 120
Yates, Tate 120
Yates, Tom 120

Memphis and Shelby County, today.

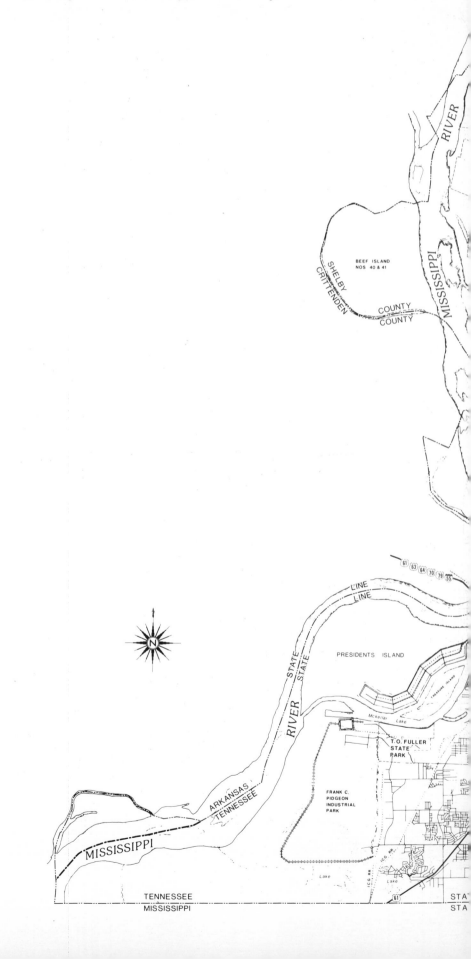